SCHOLASTIC

Math Line Designs
From Around the World

GRADES 4–6

Cindi Mitchell

NEW YORK • TORONTO • LONDON • AUCKLAND • SYDNEY

MEXICO CITY • NEW DELHI • HONG KONG • BUENOS AIRES

Teaching *Resources*

I would like to dedicate this book to Andrea Ebling. She is a first year teacher and her humor, zeal of teaching, and love of children helps to remind me why I entered this profession years ago. She has a brilliant career ahead of her and throughout the years many children will have the awesome privilege of calling her their teacher.

Editor: Mela Ottaiano
Cover design: Brian LaRossa
Interior design: Melinda Belter

ISBN-13: 978-0-439-37661-7
ISBN-10: 0-439-37661-0

2 3 4 5 6 7 8 9 10   40   14 13 12 11 10 09 08

Contents

Introduction

Welcome to *Math Line Designs From Around the World: Grades 4–6*—a collection of more than 50 interactive pages that feature designs based on motifs from different places and cultures around the world. As students complete the pages that follow, they will experience the repeated practice of essential math skills they need to help them build mastery and automaticity. To help you connect the activities in this book with your curriculum, the table of contents organizes them by skill area. You can see at a glance the activities that match the math skill you are teaching.

HOW TO USE THIS BOOK

First, students solve math problems. Then, they follow a key to determine how to color the shapes in each design to create a beautiful picture. Each page emphasizes a different math skill such as multiplication, division, fractions, and decimals. Reading the key and completing the design gives students practice with additional skills, such as following directions and recognizing patterns. Practicing basic math skills in this way helps students stay focused and motivated.

WAYS TO EXTEND LEARNING

Each activity page contains a bonus "Brain Teaser" problem, which challenges students to think about the math skill more critically. (See the answer key for solutions to these problems.)

The last three activity sheets in this book give students the opportunity to design their own math worksheets for classmates to complete. You may

want to compile these student-made worksheets into a class math design book.

Using these designs as springboards, invite students to research traditions and other aspects of the places and cultures represented in this book.

Have students continue to learn about different parts of the world through making crafts, such as Egyptian bead necklaces, Japanese origami, or Guatemalan weavings using a cardboard loom. For more ideas, see the following resources:

Art Projects From Around the World: Grades 4–6, by Linda Evans, Karen Backus, and Mary Thompson (Scholastic, 2006)

Kids Around the World Create!: The Best Crafts and Activities From Many Lands, by Arlette N. Braman (Jossey-Bass, 1999)

SPECIAL NOTE

Some of the designs in this book are related to images that have deep spiritual significance for native cultures. Remind students that art is not only decorative; explain that it can also be sacred or religious, and it is therefore important to be sensitive and respectful when creating these pictures. Please emphasize that these projects are intended to help them learn about and develop an appreciation for different cultures.

SOUTH AFRICA

Pottery Bowl

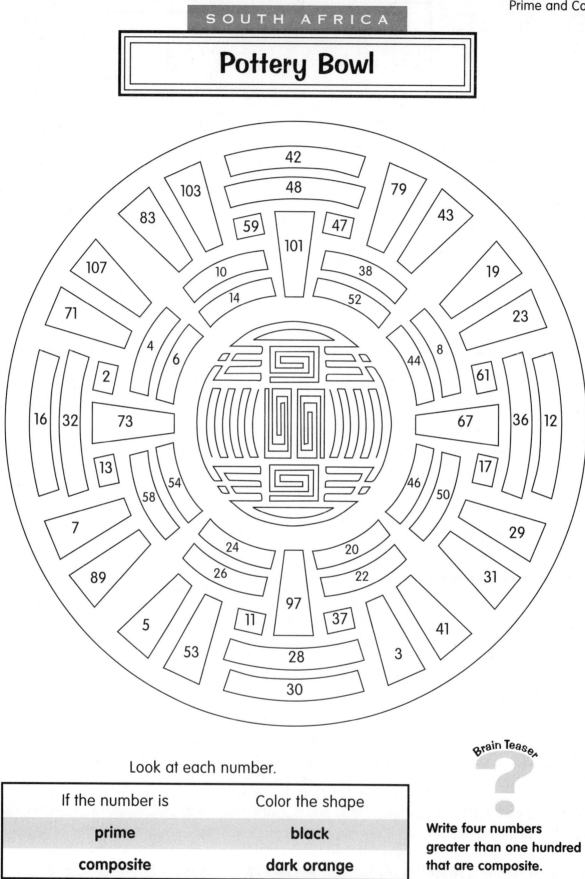

Look at each number.

If the number is	Color the shape
prime	**black**
composite	**dark orange**

Fill in the other shapes with colors of your choice.

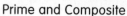

Brain Teaser

?

Write four numbers greater than one hundred that are composite.

Math Line Designs From Around the World 4–6 © 2008 by Cindi Mitchell, Scholastic Teaching Resources

Name _____

Hexagon

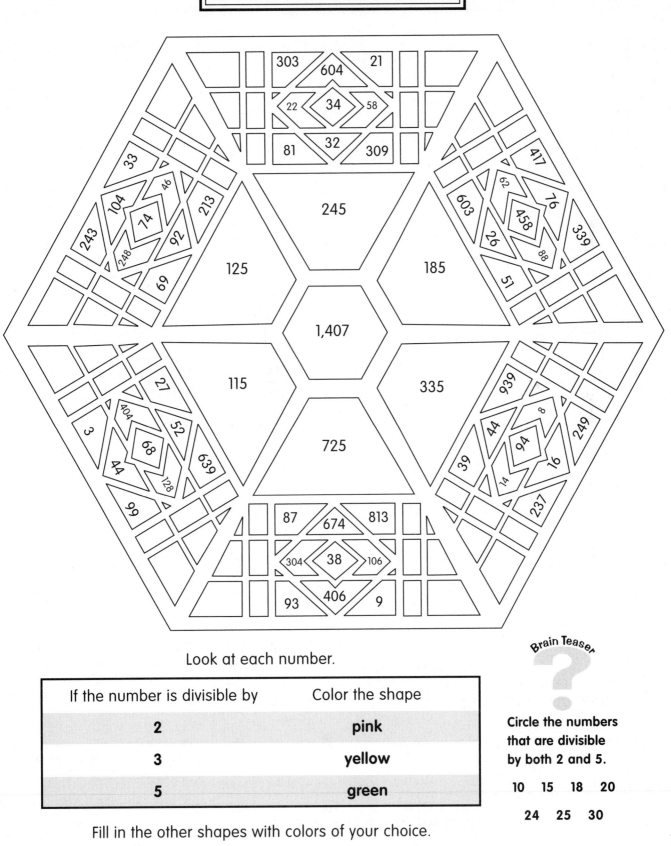

Look at each number.

If the number is divisible by	Color the shape
2	pink
3	yellow
5	green

Fill in the other shapes with colors of your choice.

Brain Teaser

?

Circle the numbers that are divisible by both 2 and 5.

10   15   18   20

24   25   30

NAVAJO

Crystals and Stripes

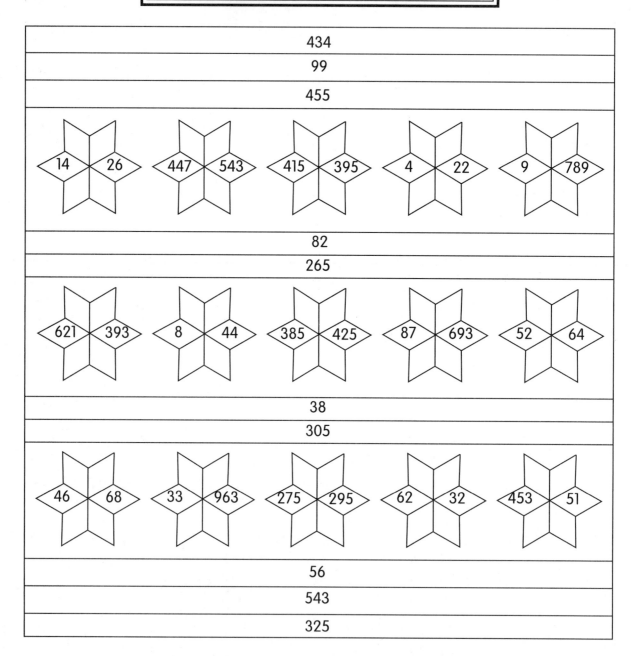

434

99

455

82

265

38

305

56

543

325

Look at each number.

If the number is divisible by	Color the shape
2	blue
3	yellow
5	gray

Fill in the other shapes with colors of your choice.

Brain Teaser

?

Circle the numbers that are divisible by 2, 3, and 5.

20   30   40   50   60

Name _____

NETHERLANDS

Decorative Plate

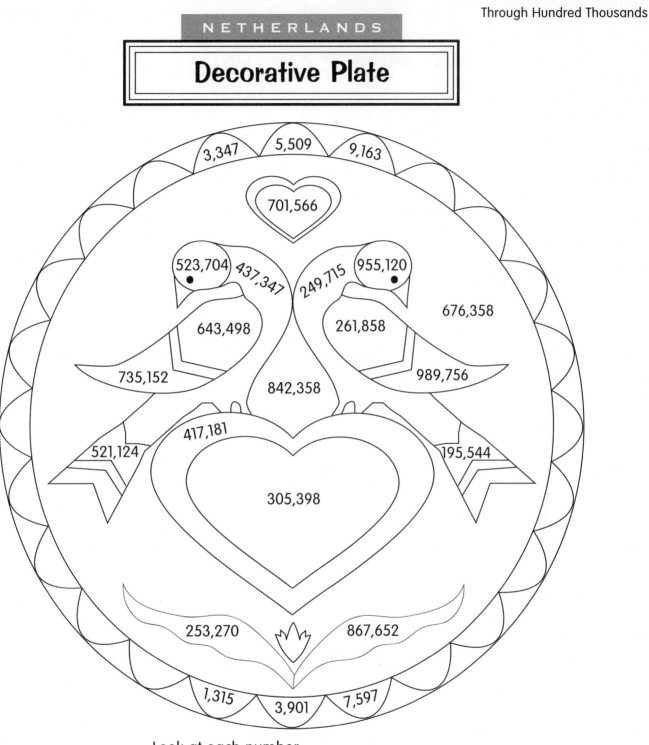

Look at each number.

If the digit in the	Color the shape
hundred thousands place is odd	**pink**
thousands place is even	**yellow**
hundreds place is even	**light green**
ones place is odd	**light blue**

Fill in the other shapes with colors of your choice.

Brain Teaser

?

Write a number that is ten thousand more than your age.

9

MAYA

Celebration Mask

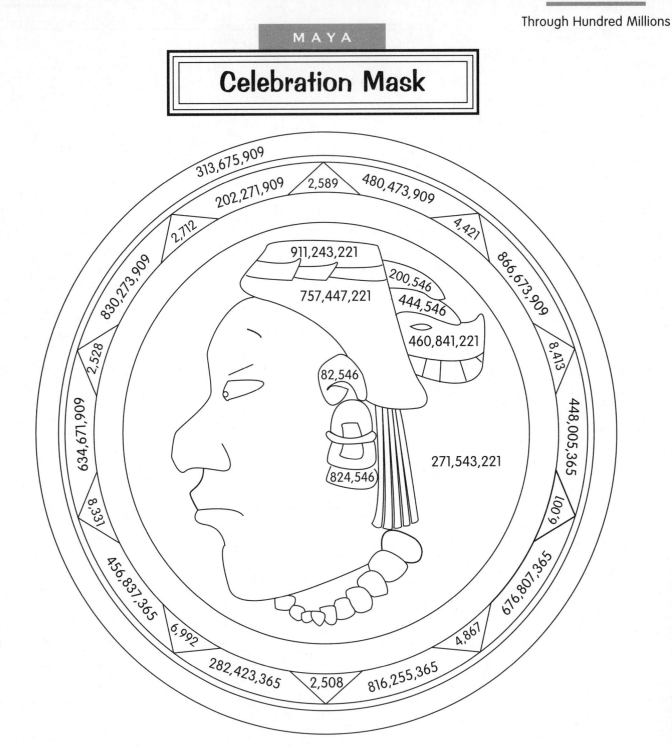

Look at each number.

If the digit in the	Color the shape
hundred millions place is odd	**black**
millions place is even	**gold**
hundred thousands place is odd	**dark green**
thousands place is even	**dark orange**

Fill in the other shapes with colors of your choice.

Brain Teaser

?

Write a number
one less than
one hundred
million.

NEW MEXICO

Twirling Rings

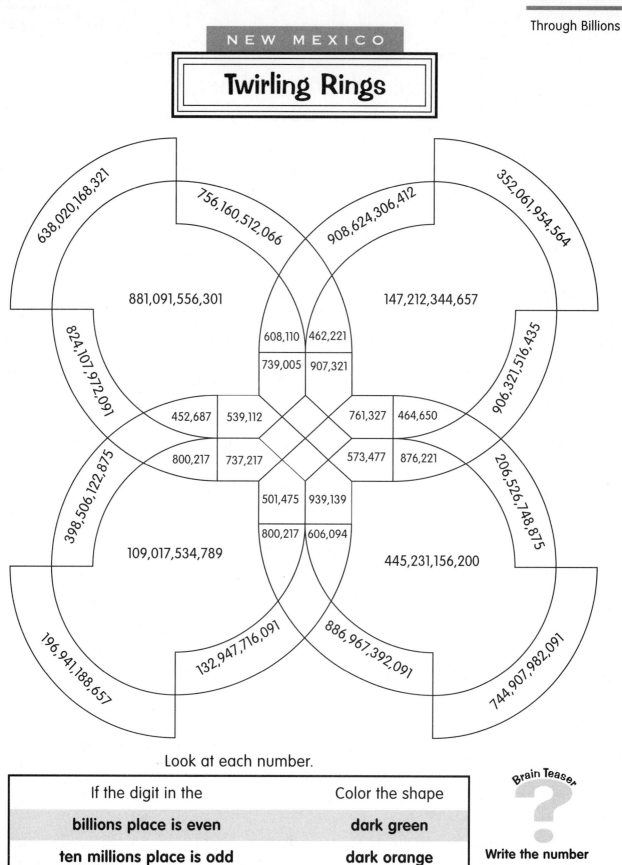

638,020,168,321

756,160,512,066

908,624,306,412

352,061,954,564

881,091,556,301

147,212,344,657

824,107,972,091

906,321,516,435

608,110 | 462,221

739,005 | 907,321

452,687 | 539,112

761,327 | 464,650

800,217 | 737,217

573,477 | 876,221

398,506,122,875

206,526,748,875

501,475 | 939,139

800,217 | 606,094

109,017,534,789

445,231,156,200

196,941,188,657

132,947,716,091

886,967,392,091

744,907,982,091

Look at each number.

If the digit in the	Color the shape
billions place is even	**dark green**
ten millions place is odd	**dark orange**
hundred thousands place is even	**brown**
thousands place is odd	**yellow**

Fill in the other shapes with colors of your choice.

Brain Teaser

?

Write the number twenty-two billion, nine hundred million, forty-five in numeral form.

CHINA

Stained-Glass Window

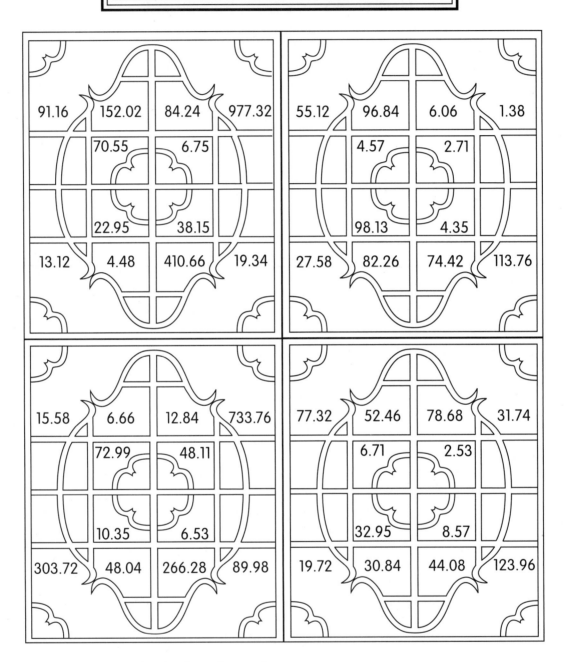

Look at each number.

If the digit in the	Color the shape
ones place is odd	**orange**
tenths place is even	**green**
hundredths place is odd	**yellow**

Fill in the other shapes with colors of your choice.

Brain Teaser

?

Write the decimal ninety-nine and four hundredths in numeral form.

RUSSIA

Blooming Flower

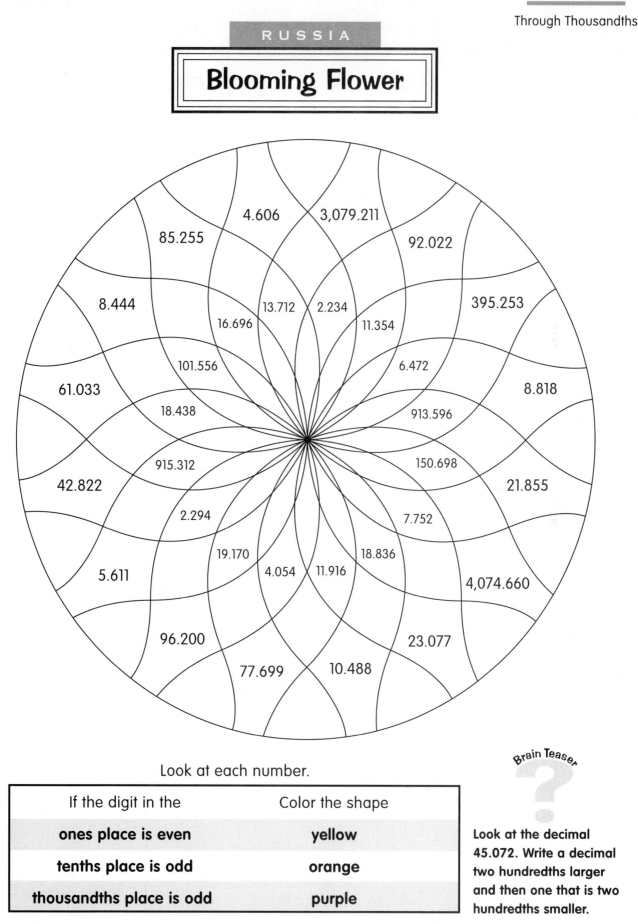

Look at each number.

If the digit in the	Color the shape
ones place is even	**yellow**
tenths place is odd	**orange**
thousandths place is odd	**purple**

Fill in the other shapes with colors of your choice.

Brain Teaser

?

Look at the decimal **45.072.** Write a decimal two hundredths larger and then one that is two hundredths smaller.

BRITISH COLUMBIA

Stripes and Diamonds

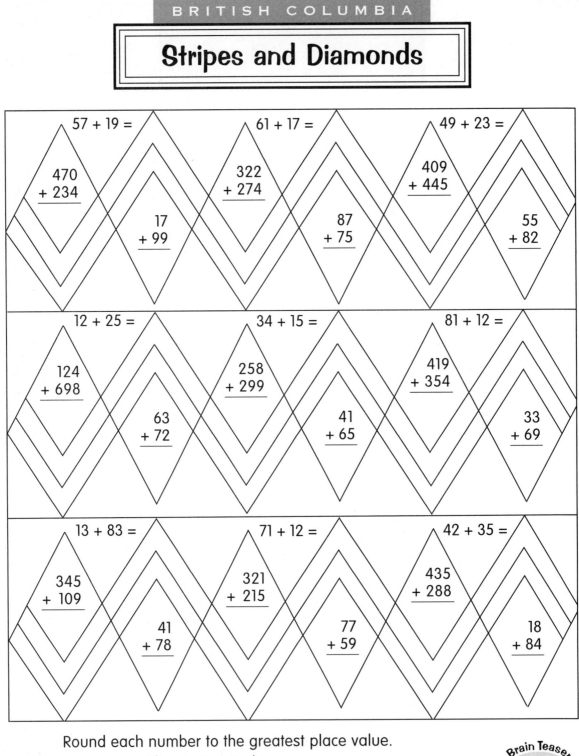

57 + 19 =

470
+ 234

17
+ 99

61 + 17 =

322
+ 274

87
+ 75

49 + 23 =

409
+ 445

55
+ 82

12 + 25 =

124
+ 698

63
+ 72

34 + 15 =

258
+ 299

41
+ 65

81 + 12 =

419
+ 354

33
+ 69

13 + 83 =

345
+ 109

41
+ 78

71 + 12 =

321
+ 215

77
+ 59

42 + 35 =

435
+ 288

18
+ 84

Round each number to the greatest place value.
Then estimate the sum.

If the estimated sum is between	Color the shape
1 and 90	purple
100 and 190	blue
200 and 800	yellow

Fill in the other shapes with colors of your choice.

14

Brain Teaser

?

There are 12 marbles
in one bag and 39
marbles in another
bag. Estimate the total
number of marbles in
both bags.

Math Line Designs From Around the World 4–6 © 2008 by Cindi Mitchell, Scholastic Teaching Resources

AZTEC

Blazing Star

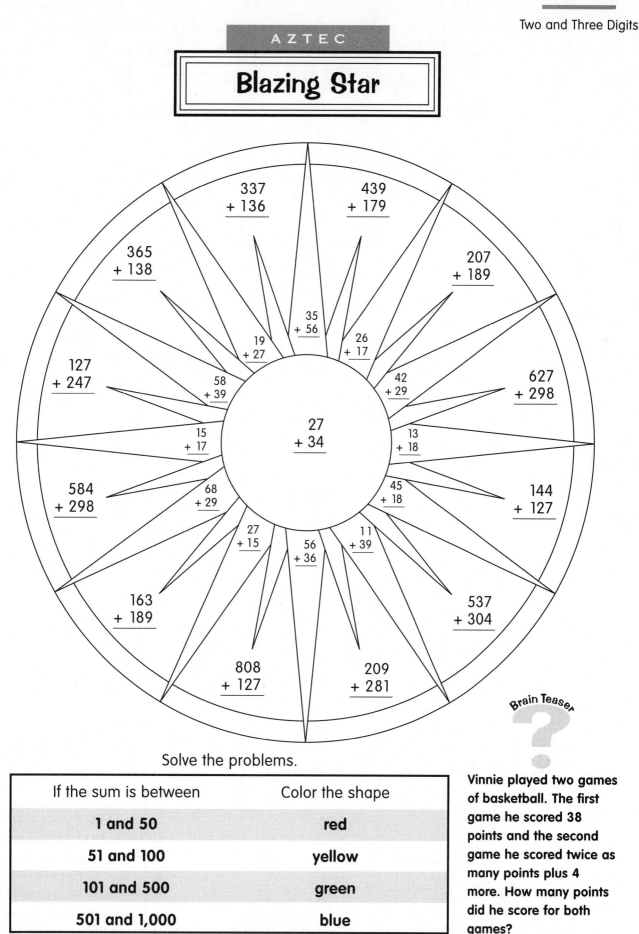

Solve the problems.

If the sum is between	Color the shape
1 and 50	**red**
51 and 100	yellow
101 and 500	**green**
501 and 1,000	blue

Fill in the other shapes with colors of your choice.

Brain Teaser

?

Vinnie played two games of basketball. The first game he scored 38 points and the second game he scored twice as many points plus 4 more. How many points did he score for both games?

JAPAN

Ancient Monolith

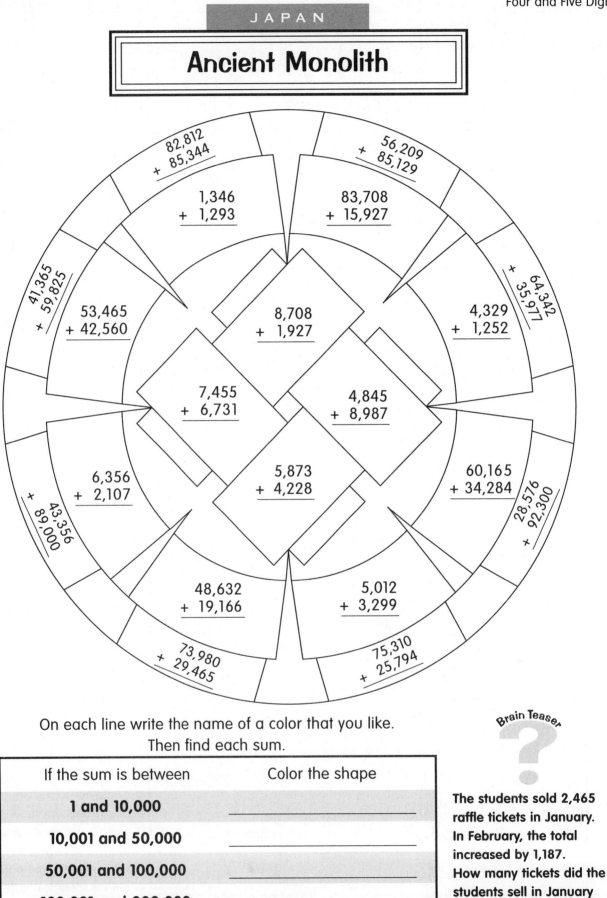

82,812
+ 85,344

56,209
+ 85,129

1,346
+ 1,293

83,708
+ 15,927

41,365
+ 59,825

53,465
+ 42,560

8,708
+ 1,927

64,342
+ 35,977

4,329
+ 1,252

7,455
+ 6,731

4,845
+ 8,987

6,356
+ 2,107

5,873
+ 4,228

60,165
+ 34,284

43,356
+ 89,000

28,576
+ 92,300

48,632
+ 19,166

5,012
+ 3,299

73,980
+ 29,465

75,310
+ 25,794

On each line write the name of a color that you like.
Then find each sum.

If the sum is between	Color the shape
1 and 10,000	
10,001 and 50,000	
50,001 and 100,000	
100,001 and 200,000	

Brain Teaser

?

The students sold 2,465
raffle tickets in January.
In February, the total
increased by 1,187.
How many tickets did the
students sell in January
and February combined?

Fill in the other shapes with colors of your choice.

Math Line Designs From Around the World 4–6 © 2008 by Cindi Mitchell, Scholastic Teaching Resources

TURKEY

Secret Passages

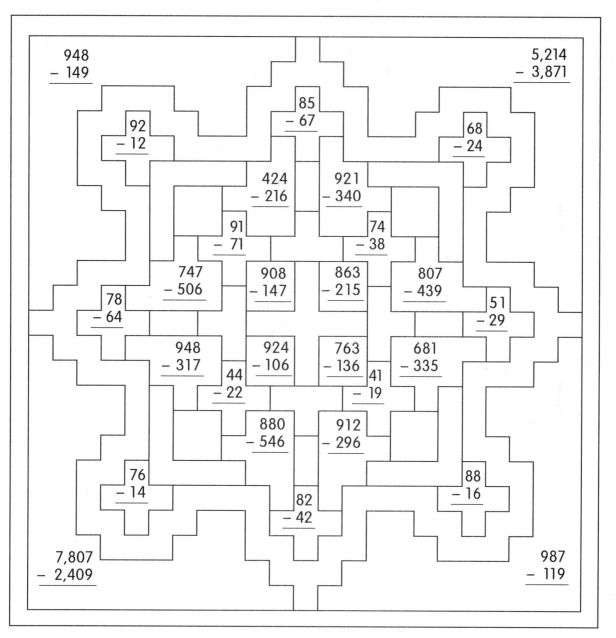

Round each number to the greatest value. Then estimate the difference.

If the answer is between	Color the shape
10 and 40	**black**
50 and 100	**yellow**
200 and 600	**green**
700 and 6,000	**purple**

Fill in the other shapes with colors of your choice.

Brain Teaser

?

Write a subtraction problem with an estimated difference of 200.

17

SPAIN

Moresque Tiles

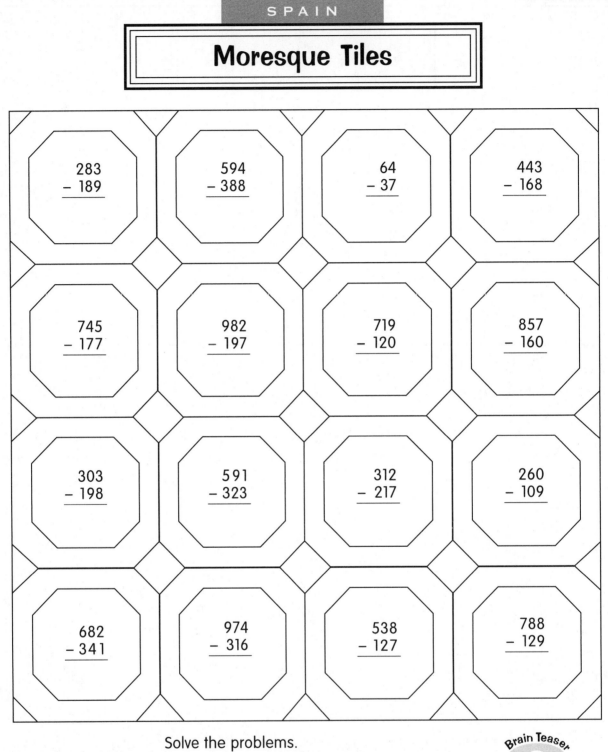

283 – 189	594 – 388
64 – 37	443 – 168
745 – 177	982 – 197
719 – 120	857 – 160
303 – 198	591 – 323
312 – 217	260 – 109
682 – 341	974 – 316
538 – 127	788 – 129

Solve the problems.

If the difference is between	Color the shape
1 and 150	**orange**
151 and 300	**red**
301 and 600	**blue**
601 and 999	**purple**

Fill in the other shapes with colors of your choice.

Brain Teaser

?

Write a three-digit
subtraction problem
with the largest
possible difference
using the following
digits: 1,2,4,5,5,9.

Name _____

CHINA

Colorful Fans

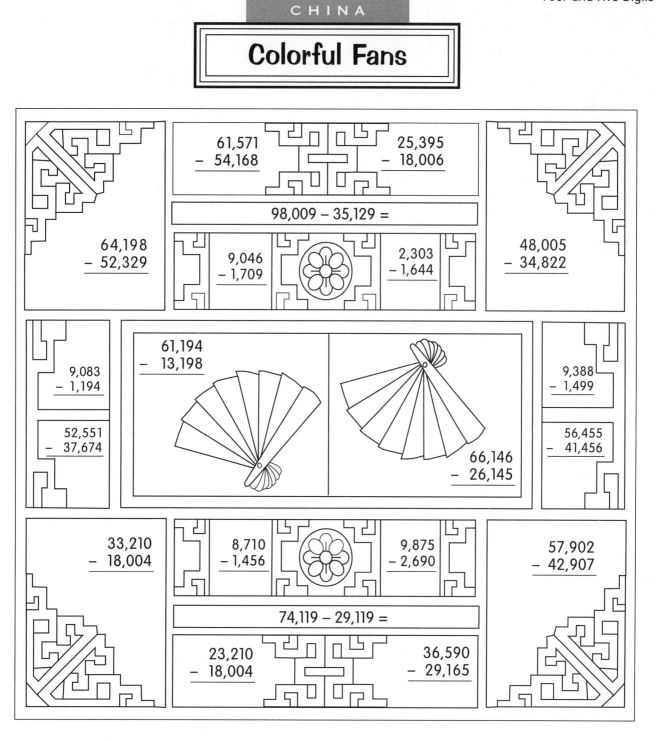

$$61,571 - 54,168$$

$$25,395 - 18,006$$

$$98,009 - 35,129 =$$

$$64,198 - 52,329$$

$$9,046 - 1,709$$

$$2,303 - 1,644$$

$$48,005 - 34,822$$

$$9,083 - 1,194$$

$$61,194 - 13,198$$

$$9,388 - 1,499$$

$$52,551 - 37,674$$

$$66,146 - 26,145$$

$$56,455 - 41,456$$

$$33,210 - 18,004$$

$$8,710 - 1,456$$

$$9,875 - 2,690$$

$$57,902 - 42,907$$

$$74,119 - 29,119 =$$

$$23,210 - 18,004$$

$$36,590 - 29,165$$

Solve the problems.

If the difference is between	Color the shape
1 and 7,500	pink
7,501 and 40,000	green
40,001 and 70,000	red

Fill in the other shapes with colors of your choice.

Brain Teaser

?

If you find the difference of two five-digit numbers, what is the largest possible answer?

19

DENMARK

Embroidered Lace

12 × 4   7 × 4   8 × 4   1 × 1   11 × 7   9 × 3   9 × 4   2 × 4

10 × 9   8 × 8

5 × 6   12 × 2   10 × 2   3 × 7

5 × 8   5 × 9

3 × 4   9 × 7   6 × 8   7 × 2

9 × 9   7 × 9

11 × 6   7 × 4   9 × 8

7 × 8   6 × 9

2 × 9   8 × 9   7 × 7   3 × 9

7 × 5   11 × 4

10 × 3   11 × 2

6 × 2   4 × 3

12 × 8   5 × 5   6 × 6   1 × 9   11 × 9   4 × 6   5 × 7   5 × 3

On each line write the name of a color that you like.
Then find each product.

If the product is between	Color the shape
1 and 15	_____
16 and 30	_____
31 and 45	_____
46 and 144	_____

Brain Teaser

?

Write three basic
multiplication
facts with the
product 48.

20   Fill in the other shapes with colors of your choice.

Name _____

RUSSIA

Twirling Rose

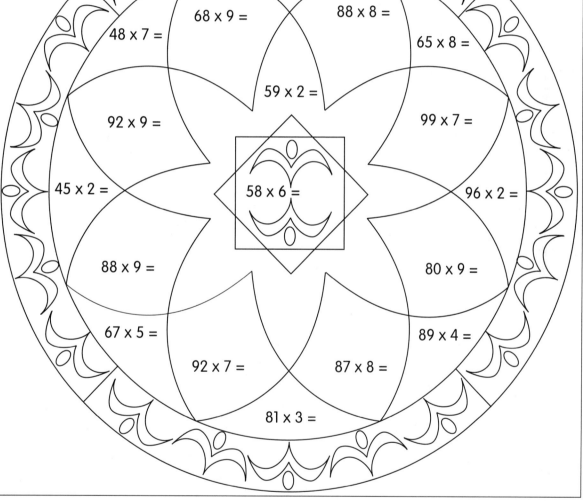

$33 \times 9 =$

$68 \times 9 =$ $88 \times 8 =$

$48 \times 7 =$ $65 \times 8 =$

$59 \times 2 =$

$92 \times 9 =$ $99 \times 7 =$

$45 \times 2 =$ $58 \times 6 =$ $96 \times 2 =$

$88 \times 9 =$ $80 \times 9 =$

$67 \times 5 =$ $89 \times 4 =$

$92 \times 7 =$ $87 \times 8 =$

$81 \times 3 =$

Solve the problems.

If the product is between	Color the shape
1 and 300	**green**
301 and 600	**yellow**
601 and 1,000	**blue**

Fill in the other shapes with colors of your choice.

Brain Teaser

?

Write two multiplication problems that each have a product of 312.

21

Name _____

MAYA

Ancient Headdress

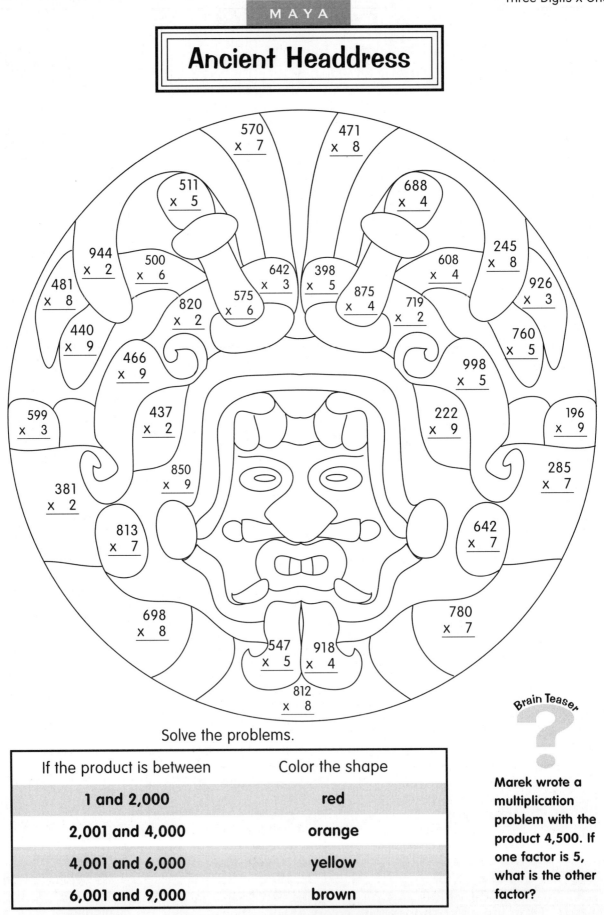

Solve the problems.

If the product is between	Color the shape
1 and 2,000	red
2,001 and 4,000	orange
4,001 and 6,000	yellow
6,001 and 9,000	brown

Fill in the other shapes with colors of your choice.

Brain Teaser

?

Marek wrote a multiplication problem with the product 4,500. If one factor is 5, what is the other factor?

JAPAN

Fragrant Blossoms

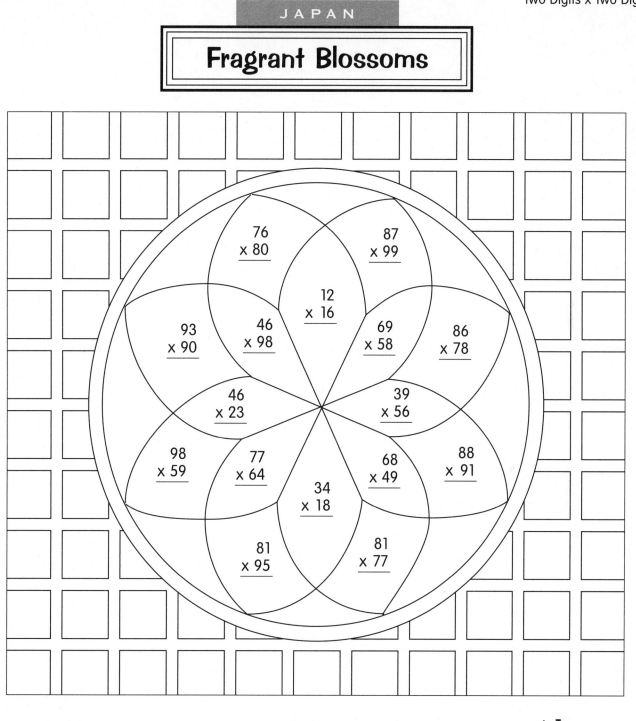

Solve the problems.

If the product is between	Color the shape
100 and 2,500	**purple**
2,501 and 5,000	**light purple**
5,001 and 7,500	**blue**
7,501 and 10,000	**light blue**

Fill in the other shapes with colors of your choice.

Brain Teaser

?

Use the following digits to create a two-digit multiplication problem with the greatest possible product: 1,2,8,9.

23

JAPAN

Fan and Waves

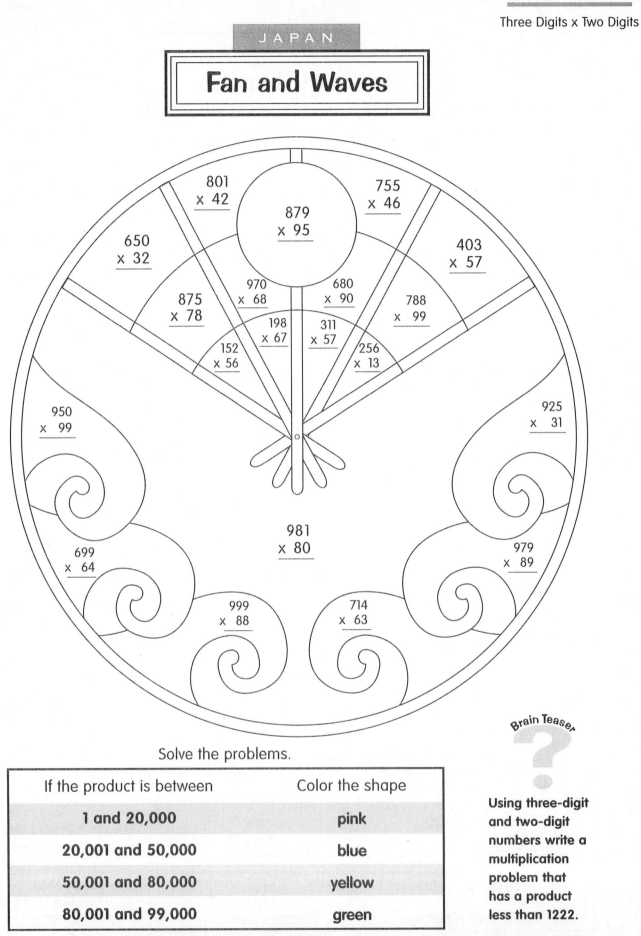

Solve the problems.

If the product is between	Color the shape
1 and 20,000	pink
20,001 and 50,000	blue
50,001 and 80,000	yellow
80,001 and 99,000	green

Fill in the other shapes with colors of your choice.

Brain Teaser

?

Using three-digit and two-digit numbers write a multiplication problem that has a product less than 1222.

INDONESIA

Ikat Wall Hanging

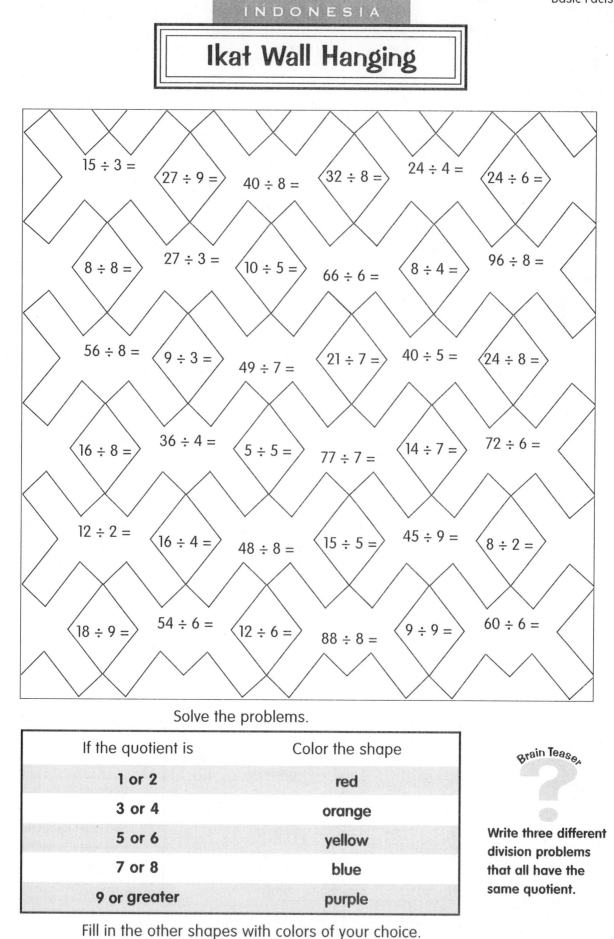

$15 \div 3 =$
$27 \div 9 =$
$40 \div 8 =$
$32 \div 8 =$
$24 \div 4 =$
$24 \div 6 =$

$8 \div 8 =$
$27 \div 3 =$
$10 \div 5 =$
$66 \div 6 =$
$8 \div 4 =$
$96 \div 8 =$

$56 \div 8 =$
$9 \div 3 =$
$49 \div 7 =$
$21 \div 7 =$
$40 \div 5 =$
$24 \div 8 =$

$16 \div 8 =$
$36 \div 4 =$
$5 \div 5 =$
$77 \div 7 =$
$14 \div 7 =$
$72 \div 6 =$

$12 \div 2 =$
$16 \div 4 =$
$48 \div 8 =$
$15 \div 5 =$
$45 \div 9 =$
$8 \div 2 =$

$18 \div 9 =$
$54 \div 6 =$
$12 \div 6 =$
$88 \div 8 =$
$9 \div 9 =$
$60 \div 6 =$

Solve the problems.

If the quotient is	Color the shape
1 or 2	**red**
3 or 4	**orange**
5 or 6	**yellow**
7 or 8	**blue**
9 or greater	**purple**

Fill in the other shapes with colors of your choice.

Brain Teaser

?

Write three different division problems that all have the same quotient.

25

Name _____

HAWAII

Meadow Flowers

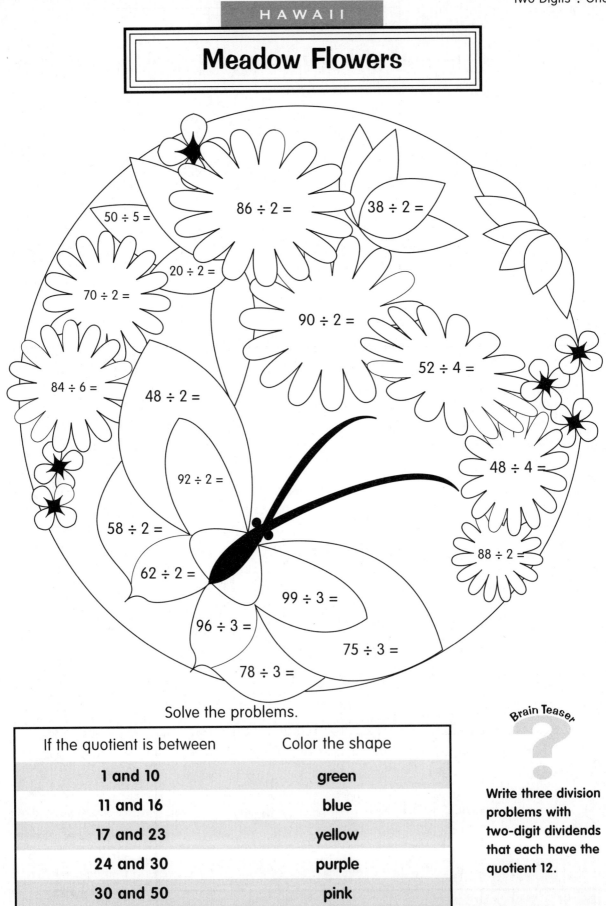

$50 \div 5 =$

$86 \div 2 =$

$38 \div 2 =$

$20 \div 2 =$

$70 \div 2 =$

$90 \div 2 =$

$52 \div 4 =$

$84 \div 6 =$

$48 \div 2 =$

$48 \div 4 =$

$92 \div 2 =$

$58 \div 2 =$

$88 \div 2 =$

$62 \div 2 =$

$99 \div 3 =$

$96 \div 3 =$

$75 \div 3 =$

$78 \div 3 =$

Solve the problems.

If the quotient is between	Color the shape
1 and 10	green
11 and 16	blue
17 and 23	yellow
24 and 30	purple
30 and 50	pink

Brain Teaser

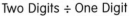

?

Write three division problems with two-digit dividends that each have the quotient 12.

Fill in the other shapes with colors of your choice.

PANAMA

Mola

368 ÷ 4 =

888 ÷ 8 =

9) 144

9) 594

4) 604

8) 232

7) 616

6) 642

5) 195

148 ÷ 2 =

309 ÷ 3 =

On each line write the name of a color that you like.
Then find the quotient.

If the quotient is between	Color the shape
1 and 50	_____
51 and 100	_____
101 and 200	_____

Fill in the other shapes with colors of your choice.

Brain Teaser

?

Find the missing digits.

X =   Y =

$$7 \overline{)X23}^{\,8Y}$$

27

Name _____

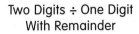

IRAN

Stars and Diamonds

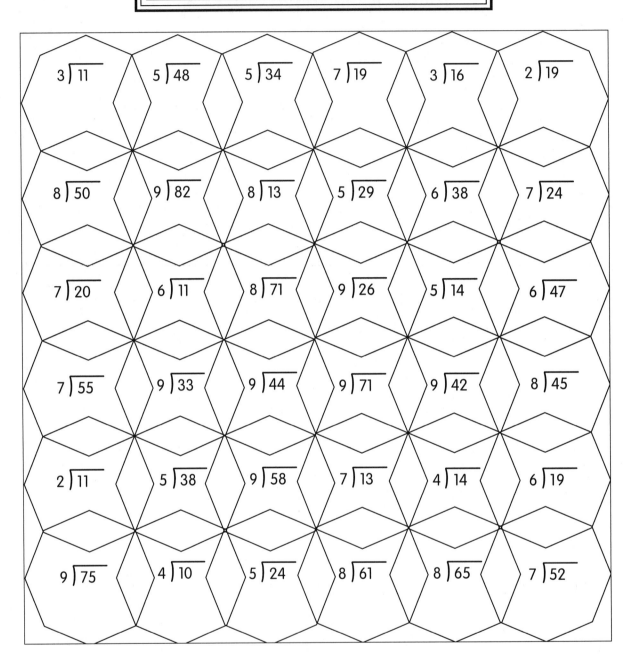

Solve the problems.

If the remainder is between	Color the shape
1 and 3	**red**
4 and 6	**green**
7 and 8	**yellow**

Fill in the other shapes with colors of your choice.

Brain Teaser

?

If a division problem
has the divisor 8, is
it possible to have
the remainder 9?
Explain.

Name _____

PERSIAN

Ornamental Flower

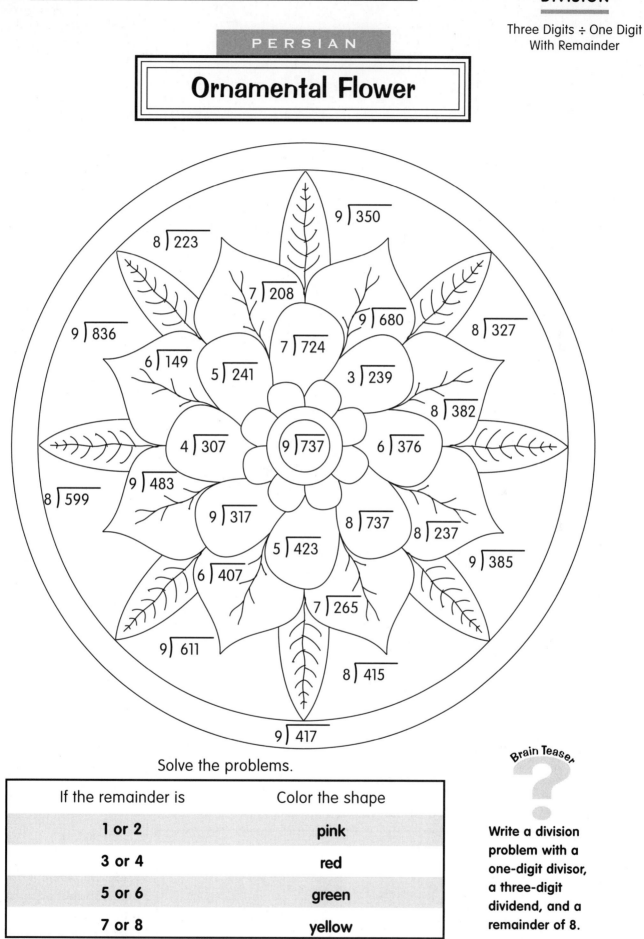

Solve the problems.

If the remainder is	Color the shape
1 or 2	**pink**
3 or 4	**red**
5 or 6	**green**
7 or 8	**yellow**

Fill in the other shapes with colors of your choice.

Brain Teaser

?

Write a division problem with a one-digit divisor, a three-digit dividend, and a remainder of 8.

29

Name _____

MAYA

Goddess

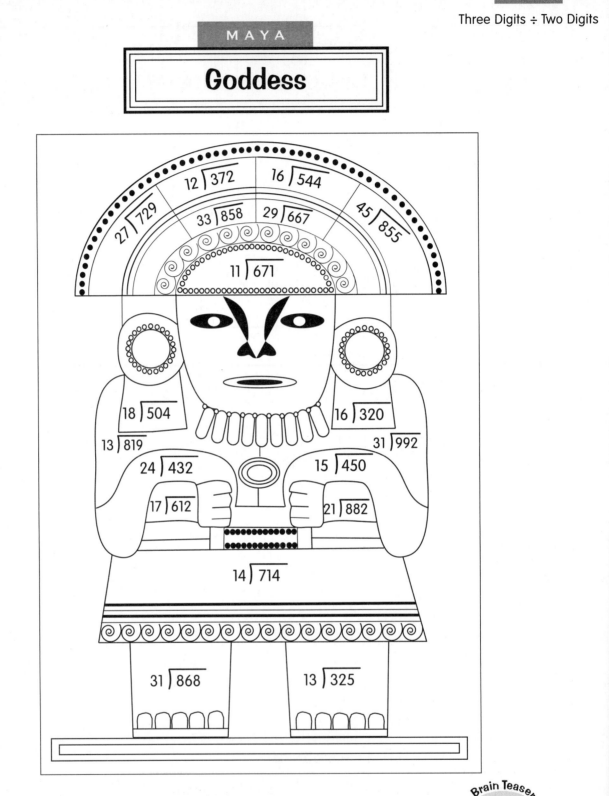

Solve the problems.

If the quotient is between	Color the shape
1 and 30	**yellow**
31 and 99	**blue**

Fill in the other shapes with colors of your choice.

Brain Teaser

?

Write two different division problems that each have a two-digit divisor, three-digit dividend, and have the same quotient.

Name _____

NORTH AFRICA

Colorful Tiles

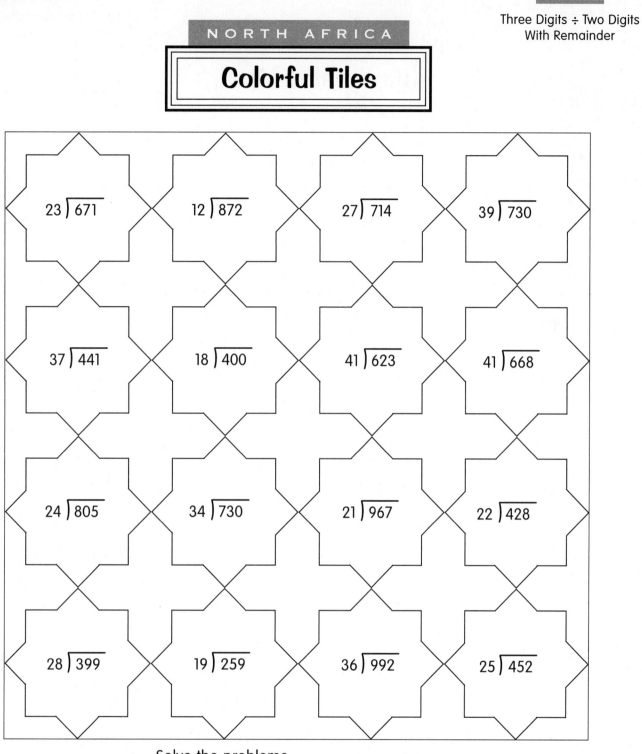

$23\overline{)671}$ $12\overline{)872}$ $27\overline{)714}$ $39\overline{)730}$

$37\overline{)441}$ $18\overline{)400}$ $41\overline{)623}$ $41\overline{)668}$

$24\overline{)805}$ $34\overline{)730}$ $21\overline{)967}$ $22\overline{)428}$

$28\overline{)399}$ $19\overline{)259}$ $36\overline{)992}$ $25\overline{)452}$

Solve the problems.

If the remainder is between	Color the shape
1 and 5	red
6 and 10	blue
11 and 15	yellow
16 and 35	green

Fill in the other shapes with colors of your choice.

Brain Teaser

?

Write a division problem with a remainder equal to your age.

Name _____

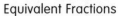

PASSAMAQUODDY

Thunderbird Mountain

$\frac{7}{8} = \frac{}{64}$ $\frac{3}{4} = \frac{}{20}$ $\frac{1}{2} = \frac{4}{}$ $\frac{9}{2} = \frac{27}{}$ $\frac{2}{3} = \frac{}{6}$ $\frac{2}{5} = \frac{}{20}$ $\frac{1}{5} = \frac{2}{}$ $\frac{8}{9} = \frac{}{18}$

$\frac{6}{1} = \frac{}{11}$ $\frac{6}{7} = \frac{}{49}$

$\frac{2}{7} = \frac{}{14}$ $\frac{6}{2} = \frac{36}{}$ $\frac{7}{8} = \frac{}{16}$ $\frac{1}{8} = \frac{}{40}$

$\frac{8}{1} = \frac{24}{}$ $\frac{5}{4} = \frac{}{12}$ $\frac{3}{7} = \frac{}{21}$

$\frac{2}{3} = \frac{6}{}$ $\frac{4}{1} = \frac{}{2}$ $\frac{2}{9} = \frac{}{27}$

$\frac{5}{12} = \frac{}{24}$ $\frac{1}{8} = \frac{}{56}$ $\frac{1}{6} = \frac{}{36}$

$\frac{4}{7} = \frac{}{14}$ $\frac{3}{8} = \frac{}{40}$ $\frac{3}{4} = \frac{}{24}$ $\frac{2}{5} = \frac{}{25}$

$\frac{8}{9} = \frac{}{81}$ $\frac{3}{12} = \frac{}{96}$

$\frac{3}{4} = \frac{15}{}$ $\frac{3}{15} = \frac{}{45}$ $\frac{2}{9} = \frac{}{18}$ $\frac{1}{7} = \frac{}{63}$ $\frac{5}{6} = \frac{}{12}$ $\frac{1}{9} = \frac{}{81}$ $\frac{4}{11} = \frac{}{33}$

Solve the problems.

If the answer is between	Color the shape
1 and 10	**red**
11 and 20	**gray**
21 and 80	**black**

Fill in the other shapes with colors of your choice.

Brain Teaser

?

Write three fractions that are equivalent to two-thirds.

32

INCA

Festive Mask

Rename in lowest terms.

If the denominator is between	Color the shape
0 and 5	**purple**
6 and 10	yellow
11 and 18	**blue**
19 and 40	red

Fill in the other shapes with colors of your choice.

Brain Teaser

?

Write a fraction that is equivalent to one-eighth when renamed in lowest terms.

Name _____

P E N N S Y L V A N I A   D U T C H

Spring Morning

Rename in lowest terms.

If the new number is	Color the shape
greater than 0 but less than 2	**pink**
greater than or equal to 2 but less than 3	light blue
greater than or equal to 3 but less than 4	yellow
greater than or equal to 4 but less than 5	light green

Brain Teaser

?

Write three improper fractions that each equal the mixed number $1\frac{1}{2}$.

34   Fill in the other shapes with colors of your choice.

TIBET

Palace Steps

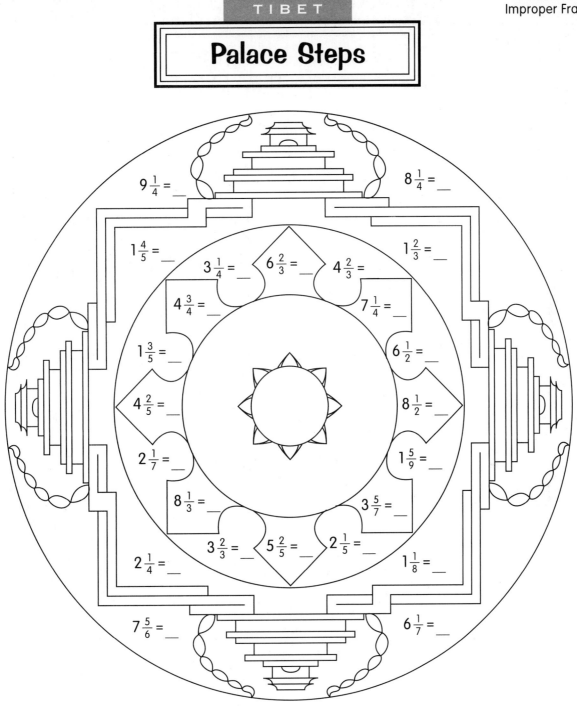

$9\frac{1}{4} =$ ___ $8\frac{1}{4} =$ ___

$1\frac{4}{5} =$ ___ $3\frac{1}{4} =$ ___ $6\frac{2}{3} =$ ___ $4\frac{2}{3} =$ ___ $1\frac{2}{3} =$ ___

$4\frac{3}{4} =$ ___ $7\frac{1}{4} =$ ___

$1\frac{3}{5} =$ ___ $6\frac{1}{2} =$ ___

$4\frac{2}{5} =$ ___ $8\frac{1}{2} =$ ___

$2\frac{1}{7} =$ ___ $1\frac{5}{9} =$ ___

$8\frac{1}{3} =$ ___ $3\frac{5}{7} =$ ___

$3\frac{2}{3} =$ ___ $5\frac{2}{5} =$ ___ $2\frac{1}{5} =$ ___

$2\frac{1}{4} =$ ___ $1\frac{1}{8} =$ ___

$7\frac{5}{6} =$ ___ $6\frac{1}{7} =$ ___

Change each mixed number to an improper fraction.

If the numerator is between	Color the shape
1 and 15	blue
16 and 30	orange
31 and 60	purple

Fill in the other shapes with colors of your choice.

Brain Teaser

?

Write three mixed numbers. Then write each mixed number as an improper fraction.

35

C H I N A

Circle of Rectangles

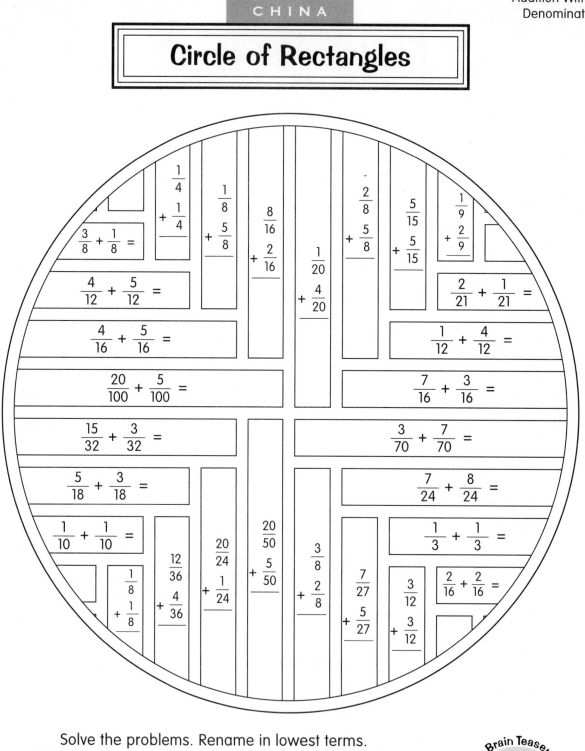

Solve the problems. Rename in lowest terms.

If the sum is	Color the shape
$\frac{1}{2}$, $\frac{1}{3}$, $\frac{1}{4}$, $\frac{1}{5}$, or $\frac{1}{7}$	blue
$\frac{7}{8}$, $\frac{5}{8}$, or $\frac{9}{16}$	yellow
$\frac{3}{4}$, $\frac{2}{3}$, $\frac{4}{9}$, or $\frac{5}{12}$	pink

Brain Teaser

?

Use fractions to write an addition problem that has a sum less than $\frac{1}{2}$.

36

Name _____

GUYANA

Geometric Pattern

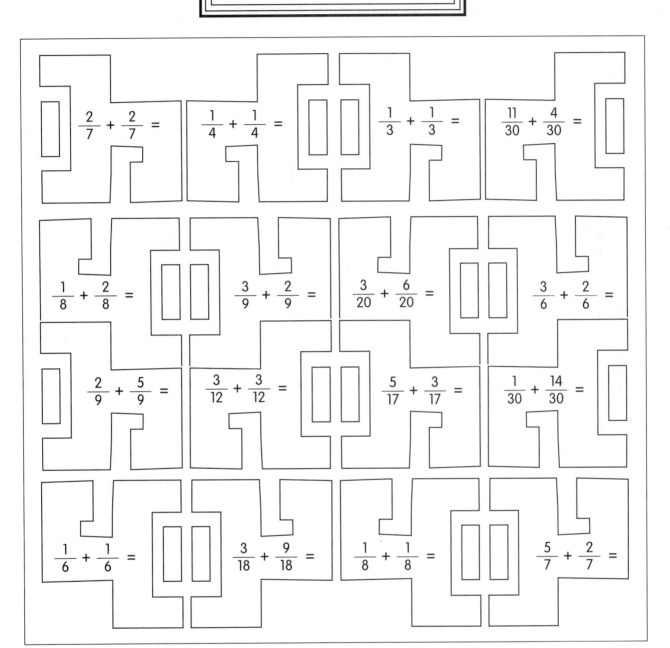

$\frac{2}{7} + \frac{2}{7} =$

$\frac{1}{4} + \frac{1}{4} =$

$\frac{1}{3} + \frac{1}{3} =$

$\frac{11}{30} + \frac{4}{30} =$

$\frac{1}{8} + \frac{2}{8} =$

$\frac{3}{9} + \frac{2}{9} =$

$\frac{3}{20} + \frac{6}{20} =$

$\frac{3}{6} + \frac{2}{6} =$

$\frac{2}{9} + \frac{5}{9} =$

$\frac{3}{12} + \frac{3}{12} =$

$\frac{5}{17} + \frac{3}{17} =$

$\frac{1}{30} + \frac{14}{30} =$

$\frac{1}{6} + \frac{1}{6} =$

$\frac{3}{18} + \frac{9}{18} =$

$\frac{1}{8} + \frac{1}{8} =$

$\frac{5}{7} + \frac{2}{7} =$

Solve the problems. Rename in lowest terms.

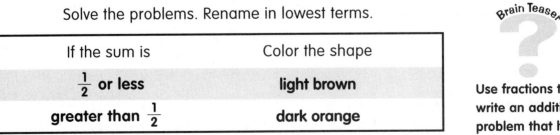

If the sum is	Color the shape
$\frac{1}{2}$ or less	light brown
greater than $\frac{1}{2}$	dark orange

Fill in the other shapes with colors of your choice.

Brain Teaser

?

**Use fractions to
write an addition
problem that has
a sum of 1.**

37

CHINA

Palace Window

Solve the problems.

If the sum is	Color the shape
$\frac{1}{2}$ or less	red
greater than $\frac{1}{2}$ and less than 1	green
1 or greater	yellow

Fill in the other shapes with colors of your choice.

Brain Teaser

?

Use fractions to write an
addition problem with
unlike denominators
that has a sum less
than 1.

Name _____

INDIA

Tile Floor

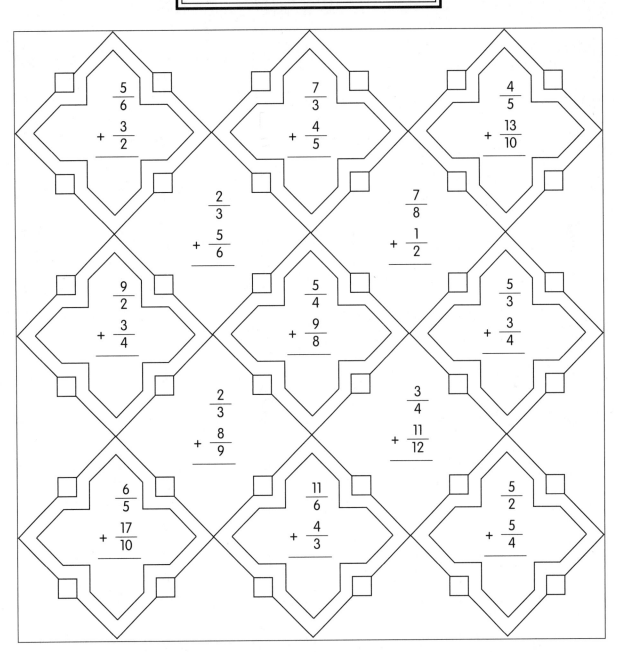

$\frac{5}{6}$
$+ \frac{3}{2}$

$\frac{7}{3}$
$+ \frac{4}{5}$

$\frac{4}{5}$
$+ \frac{13}{10}$

$\frac{2}{3}$
$+ \frac{5}{6}$

$\frac{7}{8}$
$+ \frac{1}{2}$

$\frac{9}{2}$
$+ \frac{3}{4}$

$\frac{5}{4}$
$+ \frac{9}{8}$

$\frac{5}{3}$
$+ \frac{3}{4}$

$\frac{2}{3}$
$+ \frac{8}{9}$

$\frac{3}{4}$
$+ \frac{11}{12}$

$\frac{6}{5}$
$+ \frac{17}{10}$

$\frac{11}{6}$
$+ \frac{4}{3}$

$\frac{5}{2}$
$+ \frac{5}{4}$

On each line write the name of a color that you like.
Then find each sum. Rename in lowest terms.

If the sum is	Color the shape
less than 2	_____
2 or greater	_____

Fill in the other shapes with colors of your choice.

Brain Teaser

?

**Find two identical
fractions with
the sum of $1\frac{1}{2}$.**

IRELAND

Red and Black Puzzle

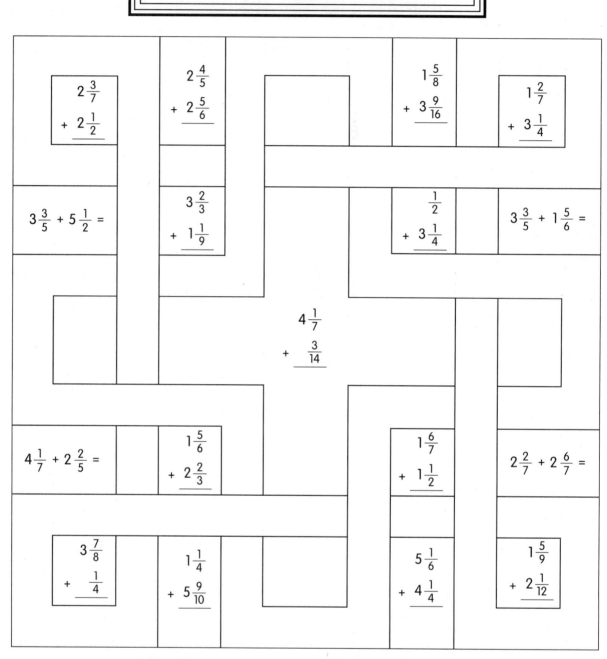

$2\frac{3}{7}$

$+\ 2\frac{1}{2}$

$2\frac{4}{5}$

$+\ 2\frac{5}{6}$

$1\frac{5}{8}$

$+\ 3\frac{9}{16}$

$1\frac{2}{7}$

$+\ 3\frac{1}{4}$

$3\frac{3}{5} + 5\frac{1}{2} =$

$3\frac{2}{3}$

$+\ 1\frac{1}{9}$

$\frac{1}{2}$

$+\ 3\frac{1}{4}$

$3\frac{3}{5} + 1\frac{5}{6} =$

$4\frac{1}{7}$

$+\ \frac{3}{14}$

$4\frac{1}{7} + 2\frac{2}{5} =$

$1\frac{5}{6}$

$+\ 2\frac{2}{3}$

$1\frac{6}{7}$

$+\ 1\frac{1}{2}$

$2\frac{2}{7} + 2\frac{6}{7} =$

$3\frac{7}{8}$

$+\ \frac{1}{4}$

$1\frac{1}{4}$

$+\ 5\frac{9}{10}$

$5\frac{1}{6}$

$+\ 4\frac{1}{4}$

$1\frac{5}{9}$

$+\ 2\frac{1}{12}$

Solve the problems.

If the sum is greater than	Color the shape
0 but less than 5	**red**
5 but less than 10	**black**

Fill in the other shapes with colors of your choice.

Brain Teaser

?

Circle each digit in the box
that could replace X in the
addition problem so the sum will
be greater than or equal to 5.

1 2 3 4 5 6 7

$1\frac{X}{8}$

$+\ 3\frac{1}{4}$

DENMARK

Pinwheel Star

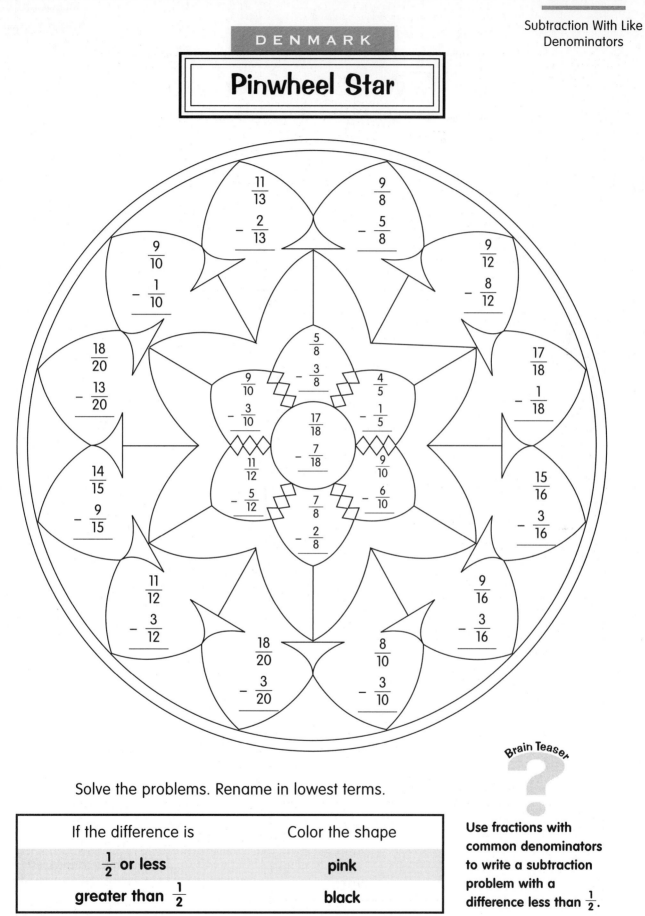

Solve the problems. Rename in lowest terms.

If the difference is	Color the shape
$\frac{1}{2}$ **or less**	**pink**
greater than $\frac{1}{2}$	**black**

Fill in the other shapes with colors of your choice.

Brain Teaser

?

**Use fractions with
common denominators
to write a subtraction
problem with a
difference less than $\frac{1}{2}$.**

AZTEC

Wall Decoration

$\frac{5}{6}$
$-\frac{2}{3}$

$\frac{7}{10}$
$-\frac{1}{2}$

$\frac{28}{30}$
$-\frac{5}{15}$

$\frac{11}{30}$
$-\frac{1}{5}$

$\frac{9}{10}$
$-\frac{3}{20}$

$\frac{17}{20}$
$-\frac{1}{4}$

$\frac{16}{21}$
$-\frac{3}{7}$

$\frac{7}{10}$
$-\frac{1}{5}$

$\frac{5}{6}$
$-\frac{1}{3}$

$\frac{2}{3}$
$-\frac{5}{12}$

$\frac{8}{15}$
$-\frac{1}{3}$

$\frac{13}{15}$
$-\frac{2}{3}$

$\frac{13}{21}$
$-\frac{1}{3}$

$\frac{7}{9}$
$-\frac{1}{3}$

$\frac{4}{5}$
$-\frac{3}{15}$

$\frac{5}{8}$
$-\frac{1}{4}$

Solve the problems. Rename in lowest terms.

If the difference is	Color the shape
$\frac{1}{2}$, $\frac{1}{3}$, or $\frac{1}{4}$	dark orange
$\frac{3}{4}$, $\frac{3}{5}$, $\frac{4}{9}$, or $\frac{1}{5}$	tan
$\frac{1}{6}$, $\frac{2}{7}$, or $\frac{3}{8}$	green

Fill in the other shapes with colors of your choice.

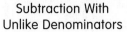

Brain Teaser

?

Using fractions with
unlike denominators,
write a subtraction
word problem.
Include the answer.

Name _____

TUNISIA

Octagon Mosaic

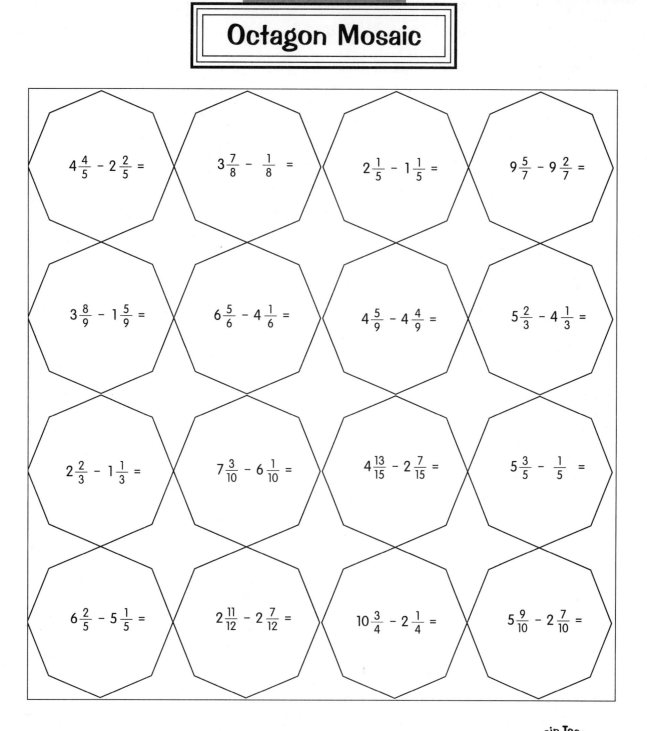

$4\frac{4}{5} - 2\frac{2}{5} =$

$3\frac{7}{8} - \frac{1}{8} =$

$2\frac{1}{5} - 1\frac{1}{5} =$

$9\frac{5}{7} - 9\frac{2}{7} =$

$3\frac{8}{9} - 1\frac{5}{9} =$

$6\frac{5}{6} - 4\frac{1}{6} =$

$4\frac{5}{9} - 4\frac{4}{9} =$

$5\frac{2}{3} - 4\frac{1}{3} =$

$2\frac{2}{3} - 1\frac{1}{3} =$

$7\frac{3}{10} - 6\frac{1}{10} =$

$4\frac{13}{15} - 2\frac{7}{15} =$

$5\frac{3}{5} - \frac{1}{5} =$

$6\frac{2}{5} - 5\frac{1}{5} =$

$2\frac{11}{12} - 2\frac{7}{12} =$

$10\frac{3}{4} - 2\frac{1}{4} =$

$5\frac{9}{10} - 2\frac{7}{10} =$

Find each sum. Rename in lowest terms.

If the sum is	Color the shape
less than 2	**purple**
2 or greater	**yellow**

Fill in the other shapes with colors of your choice.

Brain Teaser

?

Identify the
missing fraction.

$3\frac{8}{9} - 1\frac{?}{?} = 2\frac{1}{3}$

Name _____

LATVIA

Square Tablecloth

$$11\frac{7}{8}$$
$$-9\frac{1}{4}$$

$$14\frac{5}{7} - 5\frac{2}{14} =$$

$$19\frac{1}{3} - 2\frac{5}{8} =$$

$$8\frac{3}{8}$$
$$-4\frac{3}{4}$$

$$13\frac{1}{3} - 6\frac{1}{6} =$$

$$9\frac{1}{10}$$
$$-\frac{3}{5}$$

$$8\frac{3}{5}$$
$$-3\frac{1}{4}$$

$$15\frac{3}{8}$$
$$-3\frac{1}{4}$$

$$9\frac{1}{4}$$
$$-5\frac{6}{8}$$

$$9\frac{3}{4}$$
$$-\frac{1}{8}$$

$$5\frac{7}{8}$$
$$-1\frac{14}{16}$$

$$8\frac{1}{6}$$
$$-\frac{3}{4}$$

$$7\frac{8}{15} - 2\frac{1}{5} =$$

$$12\frac{2}{7}$$
$$-9\frac{1}{14}$$

$$10\frac{5}{9} - 1\frac{2}{7} =$$

$$17\frac{2}{3} - 8\frac{1}{4} =$$

$$4\frac{3}{8}$$
$$-\frac{7}{16}$$

On each line write the name of a color that you like.
Then find each difference. Rename in lowest terms.

If the answer is	Color the shape
greater than 0 but less than 4	_____
greater than or equal to 4 but less than 9	_____
greater than or equal to 9 but less than 20	_____

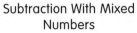

Brain Teaser

?

Fill in the missing mixed number.

$$\boxed{} - 8\frac{1}{3} = 3\frac{5}{12}$$

Fill in the other shapes with colors of your choice.

Name _____

PUEBLO

Sacred Circle

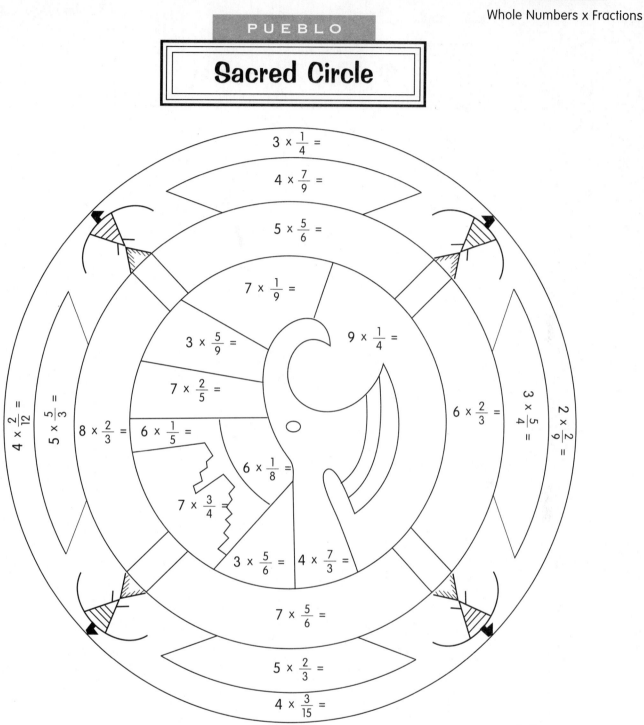

$3 \times \frac{1}{4} =$

$4 \times \frac{7}{9} =$

$5 \times \frac{5}{6} =$

$7 \times \frac{1}{9} =$

$3 \times \frac{5}{9} =$

$9 \times \frac{1}{4} =$

$7 \times \frac{2}{5} =$

$4 \times \frac{2}{12} =$

$5 \times \frac{5}{3} =$

$8 \times \frac{2}{3} =$

$6 \times \frac{1}{5} =$

$6 \times \frac{2}{3} =$

$3 \times \frac{5}{4} =$

$2 \times \frac{2}{9} =$

$6 \times \frac{1}{8} =$

$7 \times \frac{3}{4} =$

$3 \times \frac{5}{6} =$

$4 \times \frac{7}{3} =$

$7 \times \frac{5}{6} =$

$5 \times \frac{2}{3} =$

$4 \times \frac{3}{15} =$

Solve the problems. Rename in lowest terms.

If the product is	Color the shape
greater than 0 but less than 1	red
greater than 1 but less than 2	blue
greater than 2 but less than 3	yellow
greater than 3	brown

Fill in the other shapes with colors of your choice.

Brain Teaser

?

Describe in your own words how to find the product of a whole number and a fraction.

SWEDEN

Twirling Pinwheel

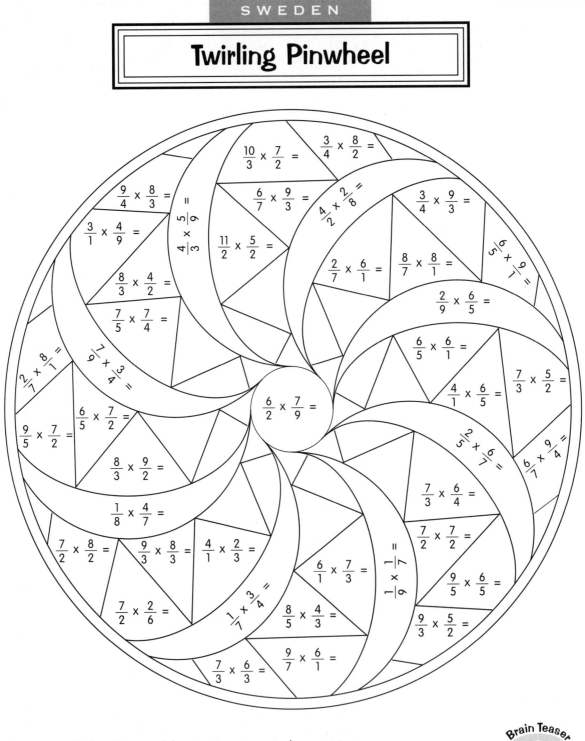

Solve the problems. Rename in lowest terms.

If the product is	Color the shape
greater than 0 or less than 1	**black**
greater than 1 or less than 5	**yellow**
greater than 5	**green**

Fill in the other shapes with colors of your choice.

Brain Teaser

?

Use fractions to write a multiplication problem with the product $7\frac{1}{2}$.

Name _____

ENGLAND

Elizabethan Bells

$3\frac{4}{7} \times 5 =$ $2\frac{5}{8} \times 5 =$ $3\frac{1}{3} \times 4 =$ $2\frac{4}{5} \times 6 =$

$2\frac{3}{4} \times 3 =$

$5\frac{1}{2} \times 2 =$ $1\frac{1}{4} \times 3 =$ $1\frac{1}{2} \times 3 =$ $4\frac{2}{3} \times 3 =$

$2\frac{1}{7} \times 3 =$ $3\frac{1}{6} \times 2 =$

$6\frac{1}{5} \times 2 =$ $1\frac{1}{8} \times 3 =$ $2\frac{1}{5} \times 2 =$ $7\frac{1}{8} \times 2 =$

$4\frac{2}{3} \times 2 =$

$6\frac{2}{3} \times 3 =$ $4\frac{1}{9} \times 3 =$ $6\frac{1}{4} \times 2 =$ $1\frac{8}{9} \times 9 =$

Solve the problems. Rename in lowest terms.

If the product is between	Color the shape
0 and 5	**blue**
6 and 10	**purple**
11 and 15	**green**
16 and 20	**yellow**

Fill in the other shapes with colors of your choice.

Brain Teaser

?

If 8 students each had $4\frac{1}{2}$ cups of cider, how much did they have in all?

P E R S I A N

Nine Stars

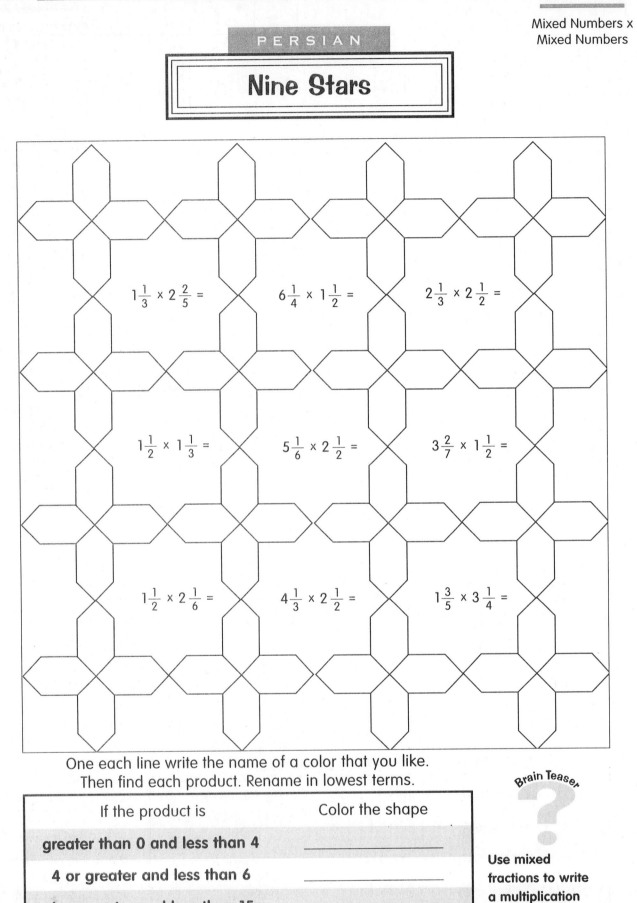

$1\frac{1}{3} \times 2\frac{2}{5} =$ $6\frac{1}{4} \times 1\frac{1}{2} =$ $2\frac{1}{3} \times 2\frac{1}{2} =$

$1\frac{1}{2} \times 1\frac{1}{3} =$ $5\frac{1}{6} \times 2\frac{1}{2} =$ $3\frac{2}{7} \times 1\frac{1}{2} =$

$1\frac{1}{2} \times 2\frac{1}{6} =$ $4\frac{1}{3} \times 2\frac{1}{2} =$ $1\frac{3}{5} \times 3\frac{1}{4} =$

One each line write the name of a color that you like.
Then find each product. Rename in lowest terms.

If the product is	Color the shape
greater than 0 and less than 4	_____
4 or greater and less than 6	_____
6 or greater and less than 15	_____

Fill in the other shapes with colors of your choice.

Brain Teaser

?

Use mixed
fractions to write
a multiplication
problem with a
product less than 5.

HOPI

Winged Warrior

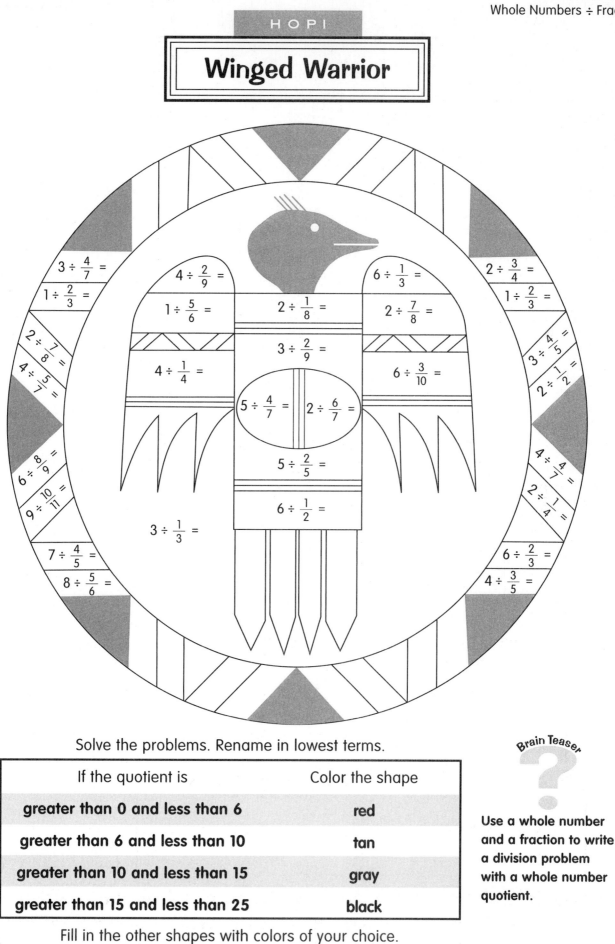

$3 \div \frac{4}{7} =$

$1 \div \frac{2}{3} =$

$2 \div \frac{7}{8} =$

$4 \div \frac{5}{7} =$

$6 \div \frac{8}{9} =$

$9 \div \frac{10}{11} =$

$7 \div \frac{4}{5} =$

$8 \div \frac{5}{6} =$

$4 \div \frac{2}{9} =$

$1 \div \frac{5}{6} =$

$4 \div \frac{1}{4} =$

$3 \div \frac{1}{3} =$

$2 \div \frac{1}{8} =$

$3 \div \frac{2}{9} =$

$5 \div \frac{4}{7} =$ $2 \div \frac{6}{7} =$

$5 \div \frac{2}{5} =$

$6 \div \frac{1}{2} =$

$6 \div \frac{1}{3} =$

$2 \div \frac{7}{8} =$

$6 \div \frac{3}{10} =$

$2 \div \frac{3}{4} =$

$1 \div \frac{2}{3} =$

$3 \div \frac{4}{5} =$

$2 \div \frac{1}{2} =$

$4 \div \frac{4}{7} =$

$2 \div \frac{1}{4} =$

$6 \div \frac{2}{3} =$

$4 \div \frac{3}{5} =$

Solve the problems. Rename in lowest terms.

If the quotient is	Color the shape
greater than 0 and less than 6	red
greater than 6 and less than 10	tan
greater than 10 and less than 15	gray
greater than 15 and less than 25	black

Fill in the other shapes with colors of your choice.

Brain Teaser

?

Use a whole number and a fraction to write a division problem with a whole number quotient.

FRANCE

Fractured Crystal

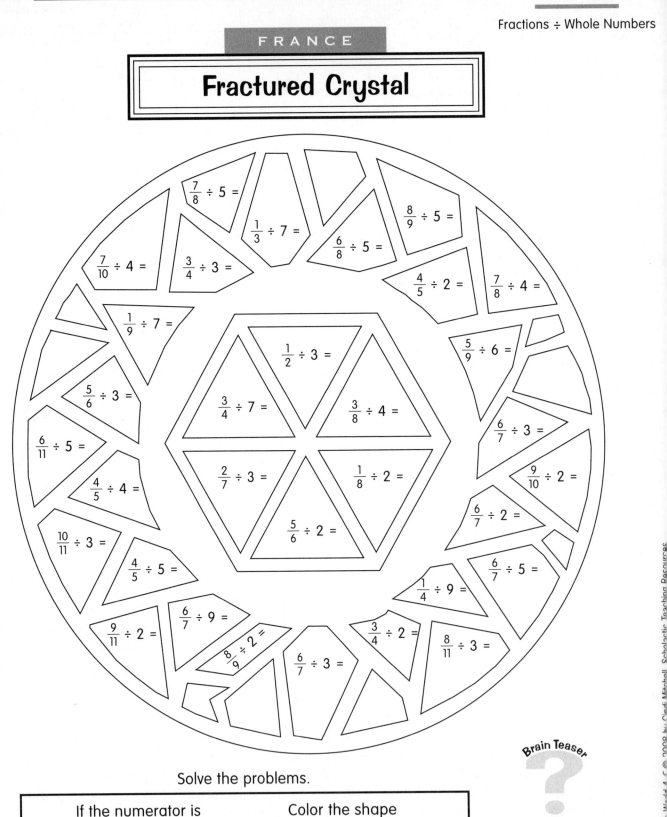

Solve the problems.

If the numerator is	Color the shape
less than 3	**red**
between 3 and 5	yellow
greater than 5	**green**

Fill in the other shapes with colors of your choice.

POLYNESIAN

Beautiful Swimmer

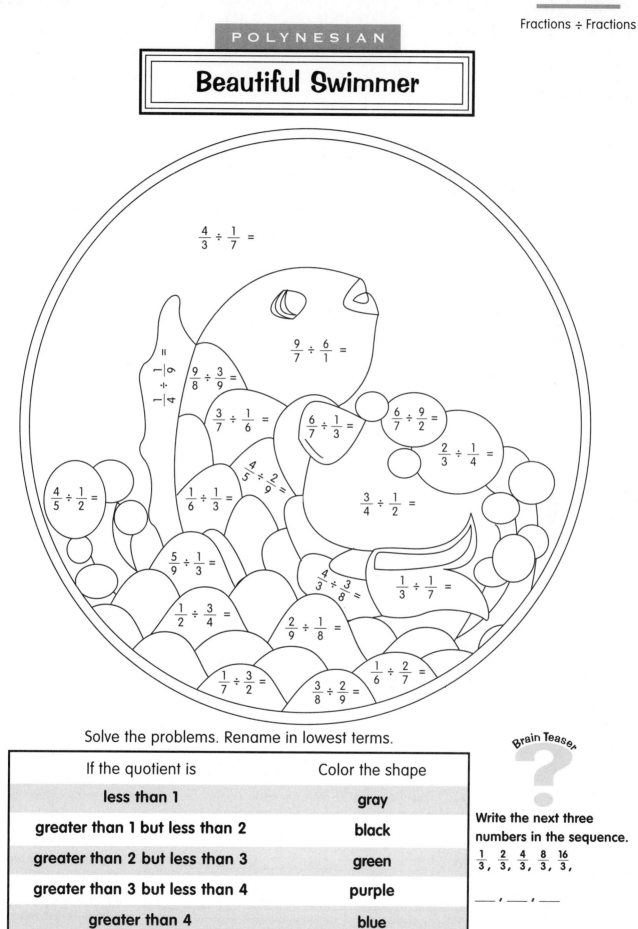

$\frac{4}{3} \div \frac{1}{7} =$

$\frac{9}{7} \div \frac{6}{1} =$

$\frac{1}{4} \div \frac{1}{9} =$

$\frac{9}{8} \div \frac{3}{9} =$

$\frac{3}{7} \div \frac{1}{6} =$

$\frac{6}{7} \div \frac{1}{3} =$

$\frac{6}{7} \div \frac{9}{2} =$

$\frac{2}{3} \div \frac{1}{4} =$

$\frac{4}{5} \div \frac{1}{2} =$

$\frac{4}{5} \div \frac{2}{9} =$

$\frac{1}{6} \div \frac{1}{3} =$

$\frac{3}{4} \div \frac{1}{2} =$

$\frac{5}{9} \div \frac{1}{3} =$

$\frac{4}{3} \div \frac{3}{8} =$

$\frac{1}{3} \div \frac{1}{7} =$

$\frac{1}{2} \div \frac{3}{4} =$

$\frac{2}{9} \div \frac{1}{8} =$

$\frac{1}{6} \div \frac{2}{7} =$

$\frac{1}{7} \div \frac{3}{2} =$

$\frac{3}{8} \div \frac{2}{9} =$

Solve the problems. Rename in lowest terms.

If the quotient is	Color the shape
less than 1	gray
greater than 1 but less than 2	black
greater than 2 but less than 3	green
greater than 3 but less than 4	purple
greater than 4	blue

Fill in the other shapes with colors of your choice.

Brain Teaser

?

Write the next three numbers in the sequence.

$\frac{1}{3}, \frac{2}{3}, \frac{4}{3}, \frac{8}{3}, \frac{16}{3},$

___ , ___ , ___

Name _____

G H A N A

Kente Cloth

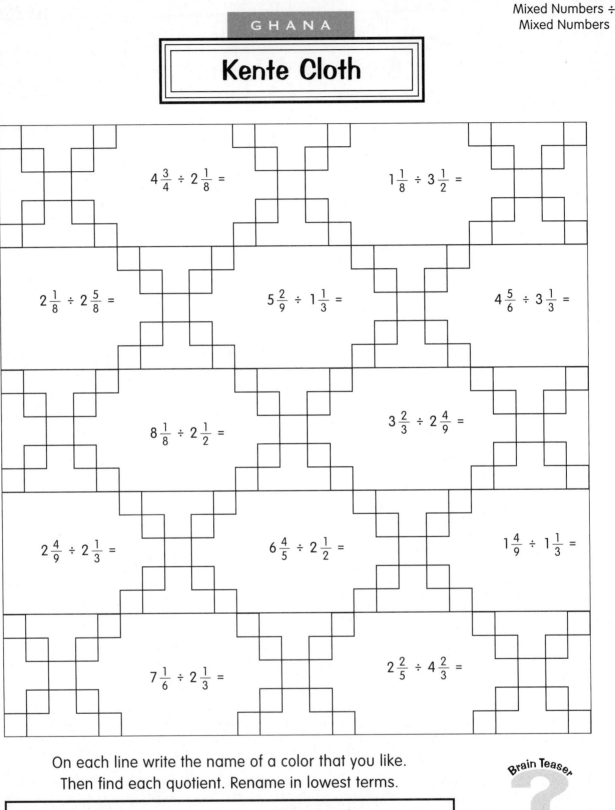

$4\frac{3}{4} \div 2\frac{1}{8} =$

$1\frac{1}{8} \div 3\frac{1}{2} =$

$2\frac{1}{8} \div 2\frac{5}{8} =$

$5\frac{2}{9} \div 1\frac{1}{3} =$

$4\frac{5}{6} \div 3\frac{1}{3} =$

$8\frac{1}{8} \div 2\frac{1}{2} =$

$3\frac{2}{3} \div 2\frac{4}{9} =$

$2\frac{4}{9} \div 2\frac{1}{3} =$

$6\frac{4}{5} \div 2\frac{1}{2} =$

$1\frac{4}{9} \div 1\frac{1}{3} =$

$7\frac{1}{6} \div 2\frac{1}{3} =$

$2\frac{2}{5} \div 4\frac{2}{3} =$

On each line write the name of a color that you like.
Then find each quotient. Rename in lowest terms.

If the quotient is	Color the shape
less than 2	_____
2 or greater	_____

Fill in the other shapes with colors of your choice.

Brain Teaser

?

Use mixed numbers
to write a division
problem with a
quotient less than 1.

Name _____

PAPAGO

Father Sun

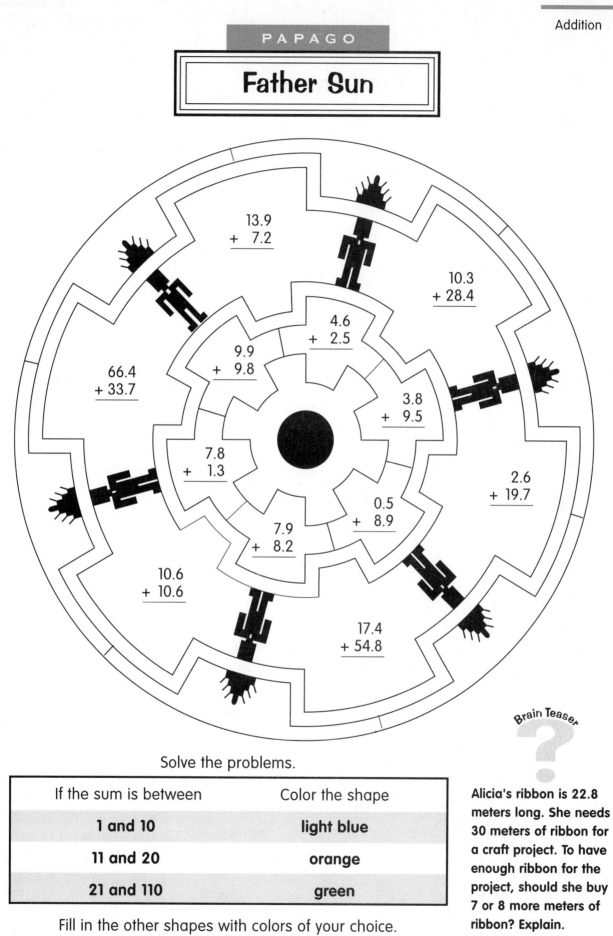

Solve the problems.

If the sum is between	Color the shape
1 and 10	**light blue**
11 and 20	**orange**
21 and 110	**green**

Fill in the other shapes with colors of your choice.

Brain Teaser

?

Alicia's ribbon is 22.8 meters long. She needs 30 meters of ribbon for a craft project. To have enough ribbon for the project, should she buy 7 or 8 more meters of ribbon? Explain.

53

PIMA

Ceremonial Bowl

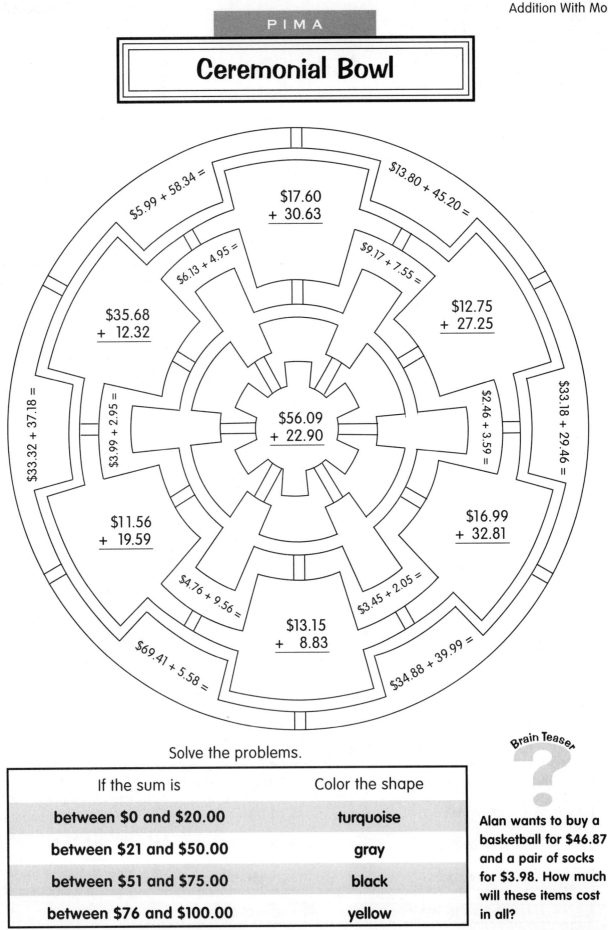

$5.99 + 58.34 =

$13.80 + 45.20 =

$17.60
+ 30.63

$6.13 + 4.95 =

$9.17 + 7.55 =

$35.68
+ 12.32

$12.75
+ 27.25

$33.32 + 37.18 =

$3.99 + 2.95 =

$56.09
+ 22.90

$2.46 + 3.59 =

$33.18 + 29.46 =

$11.56
+ 19.59

$16.99
+ 32.81

$4.76 + 9.56 =

$3.45 + 2.05 =

$13.15
+ 8.83

$69.41 + 5.58 =

$34.88 + 39.99 =

Solve the problems.

If the sum is	Color the shape
between $0 and $20.00	**turquoise**
between $21 and $50.00	gray
between $51 and $75.00	**black**
between $76 and $100.00	yellow

Brain Teaser

?

Alan wants to buy a basketball for $46.87 and a pair of socks for $3.98. How much will these items cost in all?

Fill in the other shapes with colors of your choice.

HOPI

Sun Bird

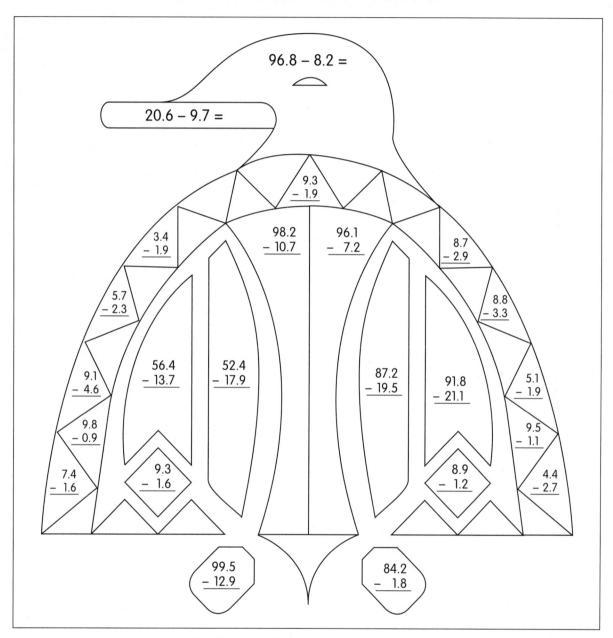

Solve the problems.

If the difference is between	Color the shape
1 and 6	purple
7 and 30	orange
31 and 80	dark blue
81 and greater	light blue

Fill in the other shapes with colors of your choice.

Brain Teaser

?

Write a decimal problem with the difference 34.

55

FRANCE

Friendship Knots

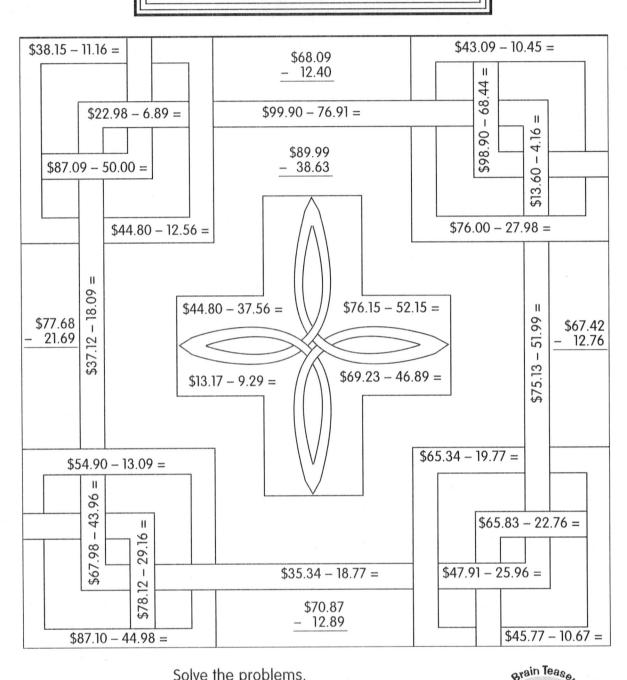

$38.15 – 11.16 =

$68.09
– 12.40

$43.09 – 10.45 =

$22.98 – 6.89 =

$99.90 – 76.91 =

$98.90 – 68.44 =

$87.09 – 50.00 =

$89.99
– 38.63

$13.60 – 4.16 =

$44.80 – 12.56 =

$76.00 – 27.98 =

$37.12 – 18.09 =

$77.68
– 21.69

$44.80 – 37.56 =

$76.15 – 52.15 =

$75.13 – 51.99 =

$67.42
– 12.76

$13.17 – 9.29 =

$69.23 – 46.89 =

$54.90 – 13.09 =

$65.34 – 19.77 =

$67.98 – 43.96 =

$78.12 – 29.16 =

$65.83 – 22.76 =

$35.34 – 18.77 =

$47.91 – 25.96 =

$70.87
– 12.89

$87.10 – 44.98 =

$45.77 – 10.67 =

Solve the problems.

If the difference is between	Color the shape
$0 and $25.00	purple
$26.00 and $50.00	pink
$51.00 and $100.00	yellow

Fill in the other shapes with colors of your choice.

Brain Teaser

?

Mavis has $39.00. Will she have enough money to buy and umbrella for $18.98 and a pair of gloves for $19.99?

Name _____

ENGLAND

London Garden

$$\begin{array}{r} 75.8 \\ \times\ 8 \\ \hline \end{array}$$

$$\begin{array}{r} 98.1 \\ \times\ 7 \\ \hline \end{array}$$

$$\begin{array}{r} 56.22 \\ \times\ 7 \\ \hline \end{array}$$

$$\begin{array}{r} 6.54 \\ \times\ 9 \\ \hline \end{array}$$

$$\begin{array}{r} 28.1 \\ \times\ 7 \\ \hline \end{array}$$

$$\begin{array}{r} 92.01 \\ \times\ 8 \\ \hline \end{array}$$

$$\begin{array}{r} 50.9 \\ \times\ 8 \\ \hline \end{array}$$

$$\begin{array}{r} 77.55 \\ \times\ 9 \\ \hline \end{array}$$

$$\begin{array}{r} 90.6 \\ \times\ 3 \\ \hline \end{array}$$

$$\begin{array}{r} 49.3 \\ \times\ 9 \\ \hline \end{array}$$

$$\begin{array}{r} 26.3 \\ \times\ 4 \\ \hline \end{array}$$

$$\begin{array}{r} 71.99 \\ \times\ 7 \\ \hline \end{array}$$

$$\begin{array}{r} 53.1 \\ \times\ 6 \\ \hline \end{array}$$

$$\begin{array}{r} 88.5 \\ \times\ 8 \\ \hline \end{array}$$

$$\begin{array}{r} 73.3 \\ \times\ 8 \\ \hline \end{array}$$

$$\begin{array}{r} 89.56 \\ \times\ 7 \\ \hline \end{array}$$

$$\begin{array}{r} 0.32 \\ \times\ 9 \\ \hline \end{array}$$

$$\begin{array}{r} 5.9 \\ \times\ 6 \\ \hline \end{array}$$

$$\begin{array}{r} 66.8 \\ \times\ 4 \\ \hline \end{array}$$

$$\begin{array}{r} 92.2 \\ \times\ 7 \\ \hline \end{array}$$

$$\begin{array}{r} 69.8 \\ \times\ 9 \\ \hline \end{array}$$

Solve the problems.

If the product is between	Color the shape
0 and 200	**purple**
201 and 400	**pink**
401 and 600	**yellow**
601 and 1000	**light blue**

Fill in the other shapes with colors of your choice.

Brain Teaser

?

When multiplying a decimal by a whole number, how do you decide where to put the decimal point in the product?

Interlocking Shapes

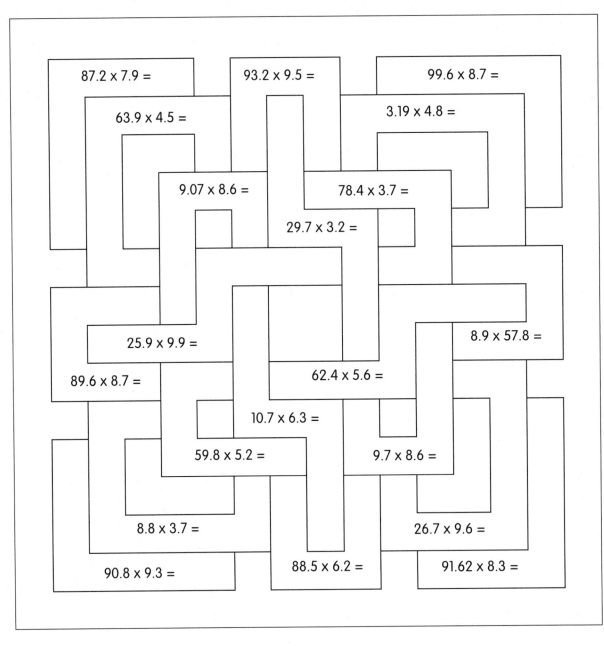

87.2 x 7.9 =

93.2 x 9.5 =

99.6 x 8.7 =

63.9 x 4.5 =

3.19 x 4.8 =

9.07 x 8.6 =

78.4 x 3.7 =

29.7 x 3.2 =

25.9 x 9.9 =

8.9 x 57.8 =

89.6 x 8.7 =

62.4 x 5.6 =

10.7 x 6.3 =

59.8 x 5.2 =

9.7 x 8.6 =

8.8 x 3.7 =

26.7 x 9.6 =

90.8 x 9.3 =

88.5 x 6.2 =

91.62 x 8.3 =

Solve the problems.

If the product is between	Color the shape
1 and 250	**light blue**
251 and 500	**yellow**
501 and 900	**orange**

Fill in the other shapes with colors of your choice.

Brain Teaser

?

Identify the missing factor.

_____ x 5.6 = 110.88

Name _____

EGYPT

Circles Everywhere

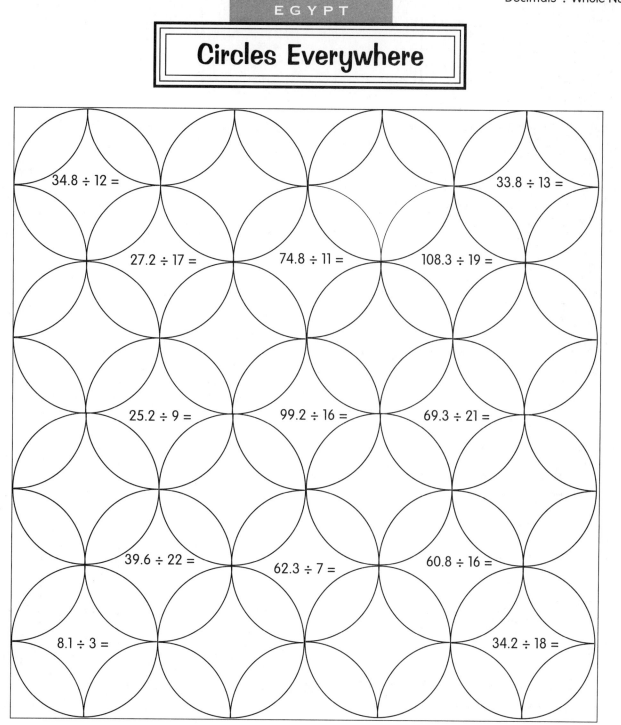

34.8 ÷ 12 =

33.8 ÷ 13 =

27.2 ÷ 17 =

74.8 ÷ 11 =

108.3 ÷ 19 =

25.2 ÷ 9 =

99.2 ÷ 16 =

69.3 ÷ 21 =

39.6 ÷ 22 =

62.3 ÷ 7 =

60.8 ÷ 16 =

8.1 ÷ 3 =

34.2 ÷ 18 =

Solve the problems.

If the quotient is	Color the shape
greater than 0 and less than 3	red
greater than 3 and less than 6	purple
greater than 6	pink

Fill in the other shapes with colors of your choice.

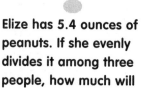

Brain Teaser

?

Elize has 5.4 ounces of peanuts. If she evenly divides it among three people, how much will each person get?

59

Name _____

Kitchen Tile

$99.12 \div 16.8 =$

$165.06 \div 13.1 =$

$39.1 \div 8.5 =$

$180.11 \div 21.7 =$

$109.76 \div 9.8 =$

$25.22 \div 9.7 =$

$35.91 \div 18.9 =$

$47.88 \div 12.6 =$

$117.45 \div 8.7 =$

$101.97 \div 10.3 =$

$59.28 \div 15.2 =$

$118.56 \div 15.2 =$

$117.6 \div 11.2 =$

Solve the problems.

If the quotient is	Color the shape
greater than 0 but less than 5	yellow
greater than 5	blue

Fill in the other shapes with colors of your choice.

Brain Teaser

?

Using decimals, write a division problem with a quotient greater than 10.

Name _____

Create a math design like the ones in this book by following these simple directions.

1. Place a math problem inside each shape in the design below.

2. Fill in the missing information in the key.

3. Give the worksheet to a friend to solve and color.

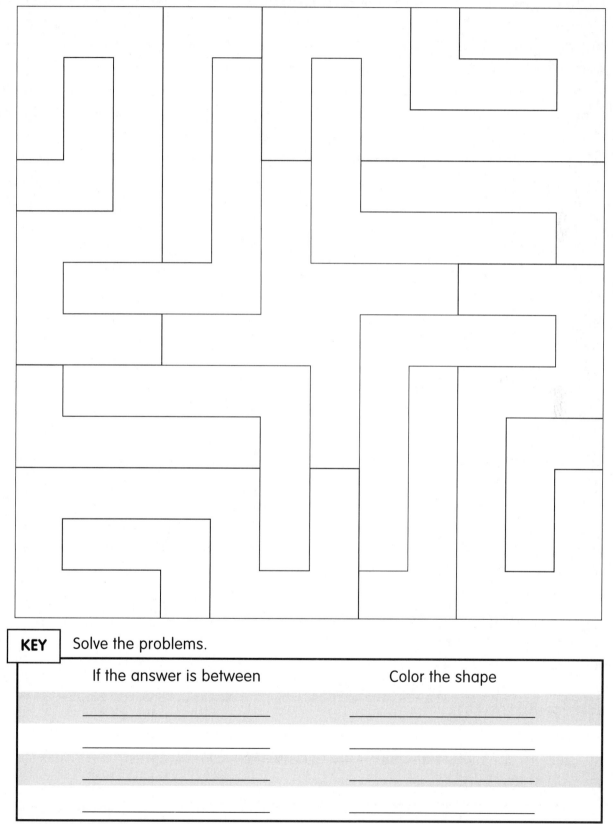

KEY	Solve the problems.

If the answer is between	Color the shape
_____	_____
_____	_____
_____	_____
_____	_____

Fill in the other shapes with colors of your choice.   **61**

Create a math design like the ones in this book by following these simple directions.

1. Place a math problem inside each shape in the design below.

2. Fill in the missing information in the key.

3. Give the worksheet to a friend to solve and color.

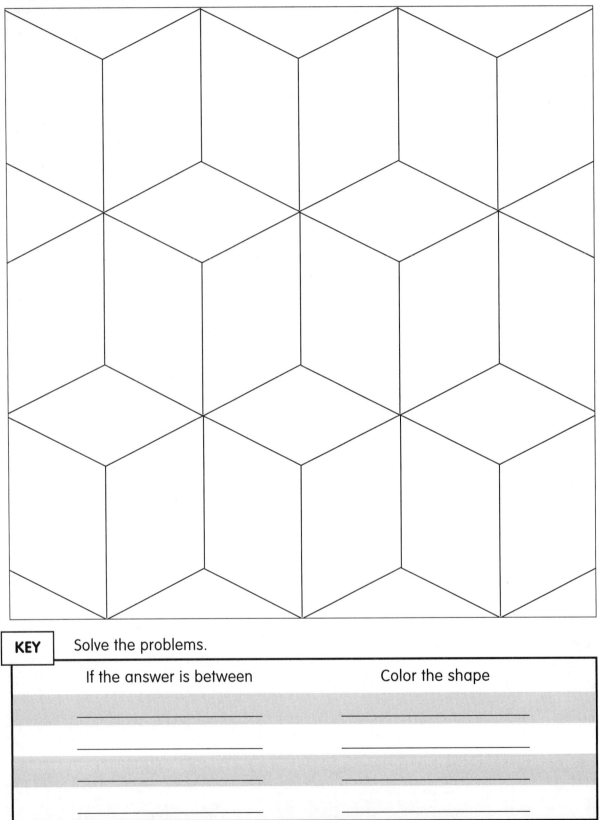

KEY	Solve the problems.

If the answer is between	Color the shape
_____	_____
_____	_____
_____	_____

Fill in the other shapes with colors of your choice.

Create a math design like the ones in this book by following these simple directions.

1. Place a math problem inside each shape in the design you draw below.

2. Fill in the missing information in the key.

3. Give the worksheet to a friend to solve and color.

KEY	Solve the problems.

If the answer is between	Color the shape
_____	_____
_____	_____
_____	_____
_____	_____

Fill in the other shapes with colors of your choice.

Brain Teaser Answers

Page 6:
Answers will vary. Example:
108, 400, 286, 755.

Page 7:
10, 20, 30

Page 8:
30, 60

Page 9:
Answers will vary. If a student is 11 years old, the number is 10,011.

Page 10:
99,999,999

Page 11:
22,900,000,045

Page 12:
99.04

Page 13:
45.092; 45.052

Page 14:
50 marbles

Page 15:
118 points

Page 16:
3652

Page 17:
Answers will vary. Example:
678 − 549 = 200 estimated difference.

Page 18:
955 − 124 = 831

Page 19:
99,999 − 10,000 = 89,999

Page 20:
Answers will vary. Example:
6 x 8, 8 x 6, 12 x 4

Page 21:
Answers will vary. Example:
104 x 3 = 312; 52 x 6 = 312.

Page 22:
900

Page 23:
91 x 82 or 82 x 91

Page 24:
Answers will vary. Example:
111 x 11 = 1221.

Page 25:
12 ÷ 6 = 2; 18 ÷ 9 = 2; 24 ÷ 12 = 2

Page 26:
Answers will vary. Example: 24 ÷ 2 = 12; 36 ÷ 3 = 12; 48 ÷ 4 = 12.

Page 27:
X = 6; Y = 9

Page 28:
No, it is not possible to have a remainder greater than the divisor.

Page 29:
The dividends will vary, but the divisor is 9. Example: 341 ÷ 9 = 37 R8.

Page 30:
Answers will vary. Example:
156 ÷ 12 = 13; 286 ÷ 22 = 13.

Page 31:
Answers will vary. Example:
496 ÷ 27 = 18 R10.

Page 32:
Answers will vary. Example:
4/6, 6/9, and 8/12.

Page 33:
Answers will vary. Example:
3/24 = 1/8.

Page 34:
Answers will vary. Example:
3/2, 6/4, 15/10.

Page 35:
Answers will vary. Example:
1 3/4 = 7/4; 4 5/6 = 29/6; 2 1/9 = 19/9.

Page 36:
Answers will vary. Example:
1/8 + 2/8 = 3/8.

Page 37:
Answers will vary. Example:
5/15 + 10/15 = 15/15 = 1.

Page 38:
Answers will vary. Example:
5/8 + 1/4 = 7/8.

Page 39:
Answers will vary. Example:
3/4 + 3/4 = 1 1/2.

Page 40:
6; 7

Page 41:
Answers will vary. Example:
4/5 − 2/5 = 2/5.

Page 42:
Answers will vary. Example: Lucas has 3/4 cup of chopped nuts. If he uses 1/3 cup in chicken salad, how much will he have left? He will have 5/12 cups left.

Page 43:
5/9

Page 44:
11 3/4

Page 45:
Answers will vary. Example: Change the whole number to a fraction. Multiply numerators and denominators. Rename in lowest terms.

Page 46:
Answers will vary. Example:
3/2 x 5/1 = 15/2 = 7 1/2.

Page 47:
36 cups

Page 48:
Answers will vary. Example:
1 1/6 x 1 2/3 = 1 17/18.

Page 49:
Answers will vary. Example:
3 ÷ 2/6 = 9.

Page 50:
Answers will vary. Example:
2/3 ÷ 2.

Page 51:
32/3, 64/3, 128/3

Page 52:
Answers will vary. Example:
1 1/3 ÷ 1 1/2 = 8/9.

Page 53:
If Alicia buys 7 meters of ribbon, she will have 29.8 meters in all. This is not enough ribbon. Although Alicia will have ribbon left over, she should buy 8 meters of ribbon.

Page 54:
$50.85

Page 55:
Answers will vary. Example:
71.3 − 37.3 = 34.

Page 56:
Yes

Page 57:
Multiply as usual. Then, beginning at the right count over as many decimal places in the product as there are in the decimal factor and place the decimal point there.

Page 58:
19.8

Page 59:
1.8 ounces

Page 60:
Answers will vary. Example:
49.5 ÷ 4.5 = 11.